Praise for

The Little Green Book on Awakening

The Little Green Book on Awakening by James George deals with large and imperative ideas. He speaks with passion and knowledge about the spiritual malaise underlying the ecological crisis facing the planet, and concludes that nothing less than an awakening of real conscience and a rapid change in human consciousness will suffice to alter the present destructive patterns in human behavior. The ecological revolution needed for a sustainable society will involve our technologies and institutions, of course, but it must also involve a radical shift in our relationship with ourselves, with each other, with other species and with the planet as a whole, in short a revolution in consciousness. This book is highly recommended to everyone interested in responsible spirituality and the quality of life on our fragile planet.

RAVI RAVINDRA, author of *Science and Spirit*

I've read your book with the strange pleasure that comes from being stimulated in such a disturbing way. You've put your all into it—and it is well worth while. Keep at it!

PETER BROOK, director, Théâtre des Bouffes du Nord, Paris

What a work! Fantastic!

MARIELLE BANCOU SEGAL, author of *The Color of Love*

What is needed above all, James George writes, is a radical awakening of our consciousness, a transformation of what we have mistakenly called human nature. This book eloquently cries out to the world for a radical blending of environmental sensibility and spiritual insight.

JACOB NEEDLEMAN, author of *The American Soul*

The
Little Green Book
on
Awakening

James George

BARRYTOWN
STATION HILL

Published by Barrytown/Station Hill Press, Inc. in Barrytown, New York 12507, as a project of the Institute for Publishing Arts, Inc., in Barrytown, New York, a not-for-profit, tax-exempt organization [501(c)(3)], supported in part by grants from the New York State Council on the Arts.

E-mail: publishers@stationhill.org
Online catalogue: http://www.stationhill.org

Cover and interior design by Susan Quasha

"Plan B 3.0" text on p. 69ff. ©2008 The Earth Policy Institute, used by permission. "The Awakening of Awareness" on p. 150-151 ©2000 Snow Lion Publications, *Self-Liberation Through Seeing with Naked Awareness,* used by permission. Al Gore's Nobel Peace Prize acceptance speech on p. 157ff. ©2007 The Nobel Foundation, used by permission.

Library of Congress Cataloging-in-Publication Data
George, James, 1918-
The little green book on awakening / by James George.
    p. cm.
ISBN 978-1-58177-112-1 (alk. paper)
 1. Human ecology—Religious aspects. I. Title.

GF80.G464 2008
205'.691—dc22

                                        2008041859

Printed in the United States of America

Acknowledgments

This book would not have been written if I had not been pushed into it by a call much stronger than my laziness. But I must also acknowledge that I have been unable to avoid the intrusion of my subjective personality into the simplicity and power of that original impulse.

Next, I acknowledge that without the love and help of my dearly beloved wife, Barbara, this book could not have been born. She has been not only my all-seeing professional editor, but my partner in clarifying and developing the ideas and practices here presented, while bearing patiently with a not even half-time husband sitting at his computer for many months.

My grandchildren, now grown up, also deserve to be acknowledged for refraining, out of the goodness of their hearts, from bitterly accusing their elders for having been asleep at the switch when the change to a sustainable lifestyle would have been both easier and cheaper for their generation than it has now become.

Since scientists are the new authorities of our endangered civilization, and since I am no scientist, I have had to rely on the kindness of many friends who are scientists and who have helped me relate my understanding of science to the great traditional religious and spiritual teachings with which I am more familiar. I cannot fail to acknowledge three of these scientific mentors: my son-in-law, Christian Wertenbaker in New York; Ravi Ravindra of Dalhousie University in Halifax, N.S., and, most of all, Lee Smolin, physicist of the Perimeter Institute in Waterloo, Ontario.

In addition, my understanding of global warming and the science related to mitigating its effects is derived primarily from Adam

Trombly, who has spent many hours over many years educating me. Chapter 12 is my acknowledgment of him as being not only a remarkable scientific pioneer but a spiritual pioneer as well.

While I was completing this book, Lobsang Lhalungpa, Tibetan scholar and teacher, died tragically in Santa Fe, N.M. Without his devoted help as friend and translator, I would have missed many wonderful opportunities in India to receive Dzogchen teachings from the greatest living Tibetan Masters. But I would have been incapable of understanding such teachings without my forty years as a pupil of Jeanne de Salzmann in the Gurdjieff Work.

Last but not least, it has been a pleasure to work with Jenny Fox of the Station Hill publishing team, and especially with my friends, Susan and George Quasha, who have made publishing a calling, rather than a business.

To all the above my grateful thanks. The shortcomings that remain in this book are mine alone. The call to awaken and to act is for everyone, for the sake of our common future. It is time for all of us to acknowledge that we must and we can. Only with that common intention can any of us face the future in good conscience, and with love, not fear.

JIM GEORGE

Toronto

October 8, 2008

Contents

For my surviving grandchildren,
Damera, Dylan, Elena, and Simon,

in memory of Carlo and Michael,

and for all those in what must, of necessity,
be the truly "green" generation.

The rapid changes in our attitude toward the Earth are also a source of hope. Until recently, we thoughtlessly consumed its resources as if there was no end to them. Now not only individuals but also governments are seeking a new ecological order. I often joke that the moon and stars look beautiful, but if any of us tried to live on them, we would be miserable. This blue planet of ours is the most delightful habitat we know. Its life is our life, its future our future. Now Mother Nature is telling us to cooperate. In the face of such global problems as the greenhouse effect and the deterioration of the ozone layer, individual organizations and single nations are helpless. Our mother is teaching us a lesson in universal responsibility.

The key point is to have a genuine sense of universal responsibility, based on love and compassion, and clear awareness.

H.H. THE DALAI LAMA

This crisis is bringing us an opportunity to experience what few generations in history ever have the privilege of knowing: a generational mission; the exhilaration of a compelling moral purpose; a shared and unifying cause; the thrill of being forced by circumstances to put aside the pettiness and conflict that so often stifle the restless human need for transcendence, the opportunity to rise.

When we do rise, it will fill our spirits and bind us together. Those who are now suffocating in cynicism and despair will be able to breathe freely. Those who are now suffering from a loss of meaning in their lives will find hope.

When we rise, we will experience an epiphany as we discover that this crisis is not really about politics at all.

It is a moral and spiritual challenge.

AL GORE

You, the individual, are the world problem. You are the only problem because all the other problems are created by your unwillingness to tackle yourself first and to understand yourself deeply and fully. The problems of the world are your problems merely magnified and multiplied.

J. KRISHNAMURTI

CHAPTER 1

Practicing the Way of NOW

In my life, I have had unusual opportunities, many of which I have wasted, to be in touch with real teachers of real teachings—those related to the WAY of NOW, to the Real that we cannot know in sleep, because the Way does not begin at that level of being. This book is my attempt to distill for myself, and for you, the non-sectarian essence of these teachings, and at the same time relate them to the most critical issue of our outer life, global warming.

Each of us has an inner life and an outer life, and it is our responsibility to see that they balance, rather than undermine one another. After all, these are the two directions in which we can apprehend reality. Though our dominant science at present tends to accept as objectively "real" only the observations of the eye turned outwards, the eye turned inwards also observes and experiences. If my inner experiences coincide with yours, and with those of others, their reality cannot reasonably be discounted as "subjective" in the pejorative sense. With a little diligence, we may even begin to understand that the same laws apply to both inner and outer worlds for the simple reason that there is only one world, and it includes both.

What matters, I believe, is not whether the eye is turned inwards or outwards, but whether one's eye is asleep or awake. At this moment, am I awake? Or am I not? The shock of this question awakens. At each instant, the answer is in the balance; and the search for truth begins when I realize that almost the entire course of my life is passed in a sleep that is qualitatively little different from sleep in bed. (For those not familiar with the terminology of waking and sleeping, I will explain what I mean later in the book.)

So long as I am merely thinking about it, no connection is made, with myself or with you, or with anything real. This kind of thinking about it can go on for years, quite uselessly. It is one-centered associative thinking. In me, "it" thinks; I am passive, asleep.

Now I see that my thoughts are just happening to me, and my other parts are not at all involved. That seeing throws a switch, and I turn my attention downward from my head to my body. I connect with the sensations of my body, just as I am at this moment. My spine is also a brain, a center, through which I move and function. Thanks to that switch of attention, I am now a two-centered being, not quite so asleep as before. I am aware of the state of my body, now. My thoughts go on, but they no longer devour the whole of my attention. I have a sense of being a little more whole, but still not fully connected with all that I am, or could be. I see that I am not whole. Naturally, I wish to be. By moments, in flashes of awakening, my heart begins to open, and an energy that was not there before stirs me from head to toe. It does not last. But, the taste of the sensation remains, the taste of "NOW I AM HERE," alive, present, vibrant.

As soon as I am again taken by my thoughts, these words about my state are empty words, with no immediate experiential content. My thoughts have separated me from my experience. I am once again in a world of horizontal relationships, all on the same level: the level of sleep. Even there, I can reconnect with the memory of another state when, for a moment, a shaft of light from the sun broke through the clouds of my sleep and penetrated my whole body with its life—now!

After such an experience, I have a new measure of what is real. Sleep is the horizontal line of successive events in time. Awakening, then, is the horizontal touched from above by the vertical, as time is touched by eternity, when all definitions are abandoned. Only then does time stand still. Only then I AM. Now. There is no other time, no other space, no other me, no other you. At last, there is no other.

My dilemma is that such an experience cannot be translated into words. Words inevitably falsify it, trivialize it, turning truth into lie, which betrays the reality of the experience. The danger is that such a betrayal can actually stop us from experiencing Now. "Sacred is secret" for this very good reason.

Yet not to write of one's life experience would be a betrayal of another kind. How does consciousness evolve if the attempt to share experiences is not made? This has most often, and most successfully, been done by the indirect methods of myth, of fairy tales, of tradition, of ritual. As our inner experience grows, we begin to understand that all of these methods are fingers pointing at the ONE, that the One is above us—yet in us. We could not exist if we were not a part of It, serving Its great purpose. Asleep, we serve involuntarily, automatically, as slaves. Awake, we still serve, but now consciously.

So in what follows we will be looking in turn at both the inner and the outer life: at the imperatives of action to avert the global warming which aberrant human behavior is inflicting on the planet, and also at the transformative awakening that alone can change that behavior in the little time remaining.

CHAPTER 2

Why Must Nature Turn Up the Heat?

Lester Brown of the World Watch Institute (and now of the Earth Policy Institute) talks about this as the time of the ecological revolution. He says it's the third revolution of our species that we know about. The first was the agricultural revolution that took centuries. The second was the industrial revolution, and that took generations. The third, the ecological revolution, is the shift from the industrial growth society to a life-sustaining society. He says that the ecological revolution is born of necessity and driven by evolutionary pressure to bring into being a sustainable civilization. But, unlike the past revolutions of our species, this has to happen in just a few years. Not only that, it has to involve not just our technologies and institutions and the systems of production and distribution; it also has to involve our values and our perceptions, who we think we are and how we experience our relationship to each other and to the world.

Joanna Macy, *Coming Back to Life*

This book is not another exhortation to ride bicycles, change light bulbs, and recycle the garbage. It has a different aim. It is for those who feel a need to understand the whole picture, including what is behind the physical canvas, visible only to the inner eye of a sensitive human being. It is for those who wish to understand the underlying issues and who see that, in order to be able to respond to the outer crisis appropriately, we must also be evolving towards an inner awakening.

Certainly I applaud the long lists of things that we all should be doing (and for the most part are not doing) to save the earth and ourselves from an ecological catastrophe. Unless we are totally insane, most of us now realize that all these things, these "doings"—the things we need to do to mitigate the effects of global warming—are necessary for our survival in the 21st century. Later in this book I have summarized some of the things we must all be doing, but the very best overview I have found on this subject is *The Hot Topic* by the United Kingdom's former chief science adviser, Sir David King, and a contributing editor for *New Scientist,* Gabrielle Walker. It gives us sober reasons for hope, while holding up the mirror to the failures of every country and almost every person to take serious action when it would have been less painful to do so.

However, I am not talking primarily about things and laws that must be changed, because I am convinced that, for there to be such a major change in human behavior, the first requirement is that we must change ourselves. Market forces encouraging technological innovation will not do it for us, and governments will not legislate boldly until the voters demand it. We need to change ourselves from inside first. As we confront the scale and urgency, increasing day by day, of the outer changes that are needed, it is surely obvious by now that a change of consciousness—an awakening—is essential, if we are to make it through this century.

The real bottom line, then, is to see that we are in a spiritual crisis that is widely misperceived as an environmental or an economic or a political or a social crisis. It is, of course, all of these; but fundamentally, when we look, either for the cause or the cure, we discover a deep spiritual crisis. And this crisis is not going to disappear through any combination that I can imagine of technological creativity, corporate reform, and rigorous governmental regulations. So it looks as if the most "inconvenient truth" is that nothing less than changing ourselves will suffice. *We must BE the change we wish to see in the world,* as Gandhi put it. The energy of a deep spiritual awakening must be joined to all the actions of the environmental activists. Nothing less will suffice to save us.

That is the thesis of this book—we must wake up. For Aldo Leopold, the father of the American environmental movement, it meant "creating a new kind of people." It's a tall order! Everything in our present culture resists it. Can we, in spite of this resistance, rise to the occasion?

"It's not enough," Vaclav Havel wrote in 1998, "to invent new machines, new regulations, new institutions. We must develop a new understanding of the true purpose of our existence on this earth. Only by making such a fundamental shift will we be able to create new models of behavior and a new set of values for the planet." And, in the same vein, Gus Speth, now Dean of Forestry and Environmental Studies at Yale, told his fellow ecologists in 2005 in Colorado:

Many of our deepest thinkers and many of those most familiar with the scale of the challenges we face have concluded that the changes needed to sustain human and natural communities can only be achieved in the context of the rise of a new consciousness. For some, it is a spiritual awakening—a transformation of the human heart. For others it is a more intellectual process of coming to see the world anew and deeply embracing the emerging ethic of the environment and the old ethic of what it means to love thy neighbor as thyself. But for all it involves major cultural change and a reorientation of what society values and prizes most highly.

No one has done more than former Vice President (and almost President) Al Gore to make millions of people around the world aware of the dangerous ways in which our collective behavior has been impacting the ecological balance of the planet. All the things on his lists of what we must do (or not do) are daunting enough without asking us, in addition, to change ourselves. Until the Live Earth concerts of July 7, 2007, he had been careful not to talk much about the need for a shift in human consciousness. Since then, he has begun speaking quite a lot about consciousness and the moral imperative of change in response to a crisis that is fundamentally a spiritual crisis. By October 12, 2007, when he heard he was to share the Nobel Peace Prize, he proclaimed powerfully that the climate crisis "is our greatest opportunity to lift global consciousness to a higher level." In a *Rolling Stone* interview later, he broadened the perspective: "There is sometimes a shift in consciousness that moves quickly and suddenly to recognize a new pattern.... That's what we're on—the cusp of now."

In his Nobel Peace Prize acceptance speech in Oslo on December 10, 2007, Gore went even further in defining what must be done in response to the present challenge:

"That means adopting principles, values, laws, and treaties that release creativity and initiative at every level of society in multifold responses originating concurrently and spontaneously.

"We need to go far, quickly....This new consciousness requires expanding the possibilities inherent in all humanity.... When we unite for a moral purpose that is manifestly good and true, the spiritual energy unleashed can transform us. The generation that defeated fascism throughout the world in the 1940s found, in rising to meet their awesome challenge, that they had gained the moral authority and long-term vision to launch the Marshall Plan, the United Nations, and a new level of global cooperation and foresight that unified Europe and facilitated the emergence of democracy and prosperity in Germany, Japan, Italy and much of the world. One of their visionary leaders said, 'It is time we steered by the stars and not by the lights of every passing ship.'"

You will find the full text of Al Gore's speech, from which the preceding paragraphs are taken, in the Appendix.

If the first awakening to reality is to realize that we must change ourselves as well as our entire energy system, the second awakening is to acknowledge that we have much less time than we thought in which to accomplish the level of change needed to avert the impending ecological catastrophe. Some of the key governments—the United States, China and India—still talk about leveling off global carbon emissions at the present levels by 2030, yet they have so far failed to reach agreement on how even that totally inadequate goal could be accomplished. The best informed scientists have been in agreement for years that stabilizing our carbon emissions at present levels will not be nearly enough.

For many months in 2007-8, Al Gore has been convening "solutions summits" of leading scientists, engineers and CEOs advising him on priorities. Finally, at Constitution Hall in Philadelphia on July 17, 2008, he challenged America and the world to awaken, since "the future of humanity is at stake." Specifically, he challenged America "to end our reliance on carbon-based fuels," and "to commit to producing 100% of our electricity from renewable energy and truly clean carbon-free sources within ten years."

There is no shortage of clean energy available from the sun and the wind. Every 40 minutes enough solar energy falls on the earth to meet 100% of world energy needs for a year. The technologies to tap into solar and wind energy are already developed and rapidly becoming competitive in cost, as the costs of oil and gas go through the roof.

Gore underlined the urgency by pointing to United States Navy data that indicates that in about five years all Arctic sea-ice is likely to melt each summer, putting more melting pressure on the massive Greenland ice cap. If both the Greenland and the

Antarctic ice sheets melt, that would mean an irreversible ocean rise of about 22 feet, inundating land now home to millions of people on every continent and eliminating some island nations.

For the last 650,000 years, CO_2 levels have been below 280 parts-per-million. In the past century, CO_2 levels in the atmosphere have risen to about 379 ppm. That is the figure given in November, 2007, by the United Nations Intergovernmental Panel on Climate Change or IPCC (who shared the 2007 Nobel Peace Prize with Al Gore). It was reached by consensus among some 2,500 of the world's top scientists, nominated by the leading national Academies of Science, after scientists from the United States had done their best to bury the most dramatic IPCC conclusions. However, if you read the complete report you will find, folded into its diagrams, the very alarming information that emissions of all green house gasses (GHG), including CO_2, had already reached 450 ppm in 2005 and may now be around 500 ppm. Remember: 350 ppm of CO_2 (or about 450 ppm of GHG equivalents) has for years been regarded in the scientific community as the prospective tipping point that we dare not exceed. It is the figure at which many governments had been hoping to cap carbon and other green house gas emissions through their gradual stabilization programs, not in 2007 but by 2030! The IPCC is telling us, as bravely as they can by consensus, that it is much worse, and it's happening much sooner than even they had expected, and that we must change course NOW. What was an ecological emergency ten years ago has now become a serious threat of global catastrophe! The growing list of endangered species now includes us.

Finally, the IPCC clearly stated that emissions must be brought down 25 to 40% below 1990 levels by 2020 to prevent truly catastrophic impacts. The lamentable target of the Canadian government in 2008 is a 20 per cent cut below 2006 levels by 2020—which, if achieved, would still leave Canada slightly *above* our 1990 total, not 25 % below. To meet its Kyoto obligations, Canada must achieve a reduction of 5% below our 1990 totals by the year 2012, and it has no chance of meeting its Kyoto or post-Kyoto obligations unless it stops developing the tar sands of Northern Alberta. If unchecked by 2011, the tar sands will produce more greenhouse gas emissions than all of Canada's passenger cars combined—five times more than needed to produce the same amount of oil from conventional forms of extraction—while destroying an area of pristine boreal forest the size of Florida, and polluting most of the Athabaska River in the process.

As Rajendra Pachauri, the Chair of the IPPC, put it at the conclusion of the November, 2007, session, "If there's no action before 2012 [when the Kyoto Agreement of 1997 expires], that's too late. What we do in the next two, three years will determine our future. This is the defining challenge." Yvo de Boer, the UN's top climate change official, emphasized the new clarity of the scientific message, adding that, while the report is not binding, now "the politicians have no excuse not to act."

Why has it taken the Intergovernmental Panel so long to come to this new sense of urgency? Some were too fearful of being labeled alarmist; some doubted their instruments when they went off the expected scale and lost time recalibrating their instruments before daring to raise the alarm; some caved in to pressure from their governments (who had paid their expenses to attend the Panel and who determine where government funding for science goes) to "soften" their analysis and not "rock the boat." In the huge Intergovernmental Panel, the consensus was always bound to understate the crisis at the lowest common denominator of alarm. In addition, it now seems evident that there has been a particularly egregious underestimation of the release of vast amounts of methane, a potent green house gas, from thawing Arctic permafrost, burning tropical forests, and the emissions of hordes of termites, cattle, pigs, and humans.

When the Nobel Committee decided to give the Nobel Peace Prize to Al Gore and the IPCC jointly, they were astutely covering both the rigorous scientific view of the Panel and the more populist Gore approach—implicitly acknowledging the necessary role each was playing in awakening global public opinion enough to force governmental action in time.

Even with this strong push from the Nobel Committee, the Bali Conference in December, 2007, was a flop, though not a complete bust. It had been intended to set in motion a process for negotiating a treaty to replace the Kyoto Protocol (expiring in 2012). Two agreements were hammered out in the final hours to keep the process going—until it becomes apparent what the next United States administration will do. The first agreement states that "deep cuts" will be needed in global emissions and calls for a binding agreement to be concluded at their next Kyoto "summit" meeting in Copenhagen at the end of 2009. The USA went along with this at the last minute.

The second agreement was a specific commitment (26 to 40% cuts in emissions by 2020 and 50% by 2050) but was limited in its application only to the 38 most industrialized countries (including a reluctant Canada) that had signed the Kyoto Protocol. The United States did not sign the Kyoto Protocol and is therefore not bound by it. China and India were among the 176 Kyoto signatories but are not among the most industrialized countries. The scope of this second agreement is therefore minimal, since three of the largest polluters are not committed to it.

The biggest polluter, as Al Gore ruefully said of his own country at Bali, is the biggest problem. But, as he also said—and with more enthusiasm—that could soon change. All the major players are waiting to see what happens in the U.S. elections in November, 2008, so real action cannot be expected before 2009. Another critical year lost.

The Europeans did not get their demand that the guidelines for the serious negotiations of 2009 should include mandatory emissions targets that all countries must meet by 2020. China attended but took little part in the Conference. The United States joined the consensus only after it was watered down to an agreement to negotiate a replacement arrangement by 2009, but with no mandatory targets.

In the light of the very slim progress made at Bali, it is worth noting that even our best scientists' worst case scenarios of CO_2-GHG emissions and Arctic ice depletion have been seriously underestimating the time we now know we have in which to change course. We can already see the mayhem that these unanticipated GHG emissions are causing and we know that it is rapidly getting worse. Climate stability is quickly deteriorating and the rate of deterioration is increasing, even at present CO_2

levels. If we choose to ignore the warnings of science, we (or our descendants) will pay a high price. The truth is that instead of aiming at holding our emissions to present levels, we must actually reduce global carbon emissions to zero within 10 to 20 years, so as to have some hope of holding CO_2 levels to 400 ppm in this century.

This grim message was driven home by NASA's top environmental scientist, Dr. Jim Hansen, Director of the Goddard Institute of Space Sciences, when he appeared before the House Select Committee on Energy Independence and Global Warming in June, 2008. Unless the U.S. begins to act soon, he pointed out, "it will become impractical to constrain atmospheric carbon dioxide, the greenhouse gas produced in burning fossil fuels, to a level that prevents the climate system from passing tipping points that lead to disastrous climate changes that spiral dynamically out of humanity's control. We're toast if we don't get on a very different path. This is the last chance."

The most important action to take now, Dr. Hansen recommended, "is to block coal-fired power plants." The technology needed for effective carbon sequestration for so-called "clean coal" plants is still far from affordable in either energy or money. Hansen placed special blame on the "CEOs of fossil energy companies [who] know what they are doing and are aware of [the] long-term consequences of continued business as usual." In his opinion, they should "be tried for high crimes against humanity and nature! I anticipate testifying against relevant CEOs in future public trials."

Scientists from the National Center for Atmospheric Research in Boulder, the University of Colorado, and McGill University in Montreal drove home this point in April, 2008, with a critique in *Nature* of the Intergovernmental Panel on Climate Change's "dangerous assumptions" that most of the changes necessary to mitigate global warming will occur spontaneously, through technological innovation, without the need for rigorous laws requiring the decarbonization of the energy economy. These scientists said that the IPCC was "playing a risky game" in making this assumption, which runs counter to much current evidence. "We are moving in the opposite direction right now."

If even the IPCC is not giving us the unvarnished truth, how can we hold voters responsible for electing legislators bold enough to take decisive action? This is not an academic question. In 2009, the incoming President of the United States will have an awesome responsibility to get things moving quickly. Canada is also likely to have an election in 2009 or sooner, and it is shaping up as the first of many "Green Shift" elections, with the Liberal Opposition leader Stephane Dion proposing, in June, 2008, serious progressive carbon taxes with roughly equal offsetting income tax cuts. From my ecological perspective, carbon taxation is the only honest way to deal with the requirement to cut CO_2 emissions. Most business interests would prefer cap and trade schemes that would place fewer burdens on corporations, but, while cap and trade may be a useful complement to carbon taxation (or a carbon auction, as Oliver Tickell proposes in *Kyoto 2*), it would be a disastrous substitute. Most

Canadians, even in Alberta, want federal government action to cap and reduce emissions, but whether these Canadians will be "green" enough to vote for making energy more expensive and slowing down tar sands development remains to be seen.

Naturally, no one country wants either to lead the parade or to fall too far behind the global consensus. Therefore the entire world must be mobilized as rapidly as for global war. We are in a global battle for the survival of human life and everyone is equally threatened. Every aspect of civil society in every culture and every continent must be mobilized—all are at risk.

Within the environmental movement, one of our global priorities must be to make the largely secular "green" movement into a spiritual/green movement, acknowledging that we are facing a crisis that is both spiritual and ecological. Only in that way can this movement become global, for the rest of the world is not as secular as the so-called West. To confront the challenges of global warming, we need Asia and the Middle East, Africa and South America—not just the economically developed countries.

The integration of the spiritual and the environmental movements is the most urgent next step towards an unstoppable global movement in response to a crisis that threatens the entire planet. In the West, the "greens" have been dismissive in their attitude towards the spiritual disciplines, accusing practitioners of "sitting on their cushions" rather than joining in protest rallies. Yet, in most of the rest of the world, spiritual duties have precedence over secular obligations. In facing the common crisis, both streams have a common need to work together, recognizing the validity of both outer and inner actions aimed at saving our one world.

As an example of the sort of inner actions I am upholding, let me take you back a few years to a Threshold Foundation Conference we held at Saratoga Springs, New York, with Oren Lyons, a Chief of the Onondaga tribe based near Syracuse. When I noticed that Oren was getting up long before the rest of us each morning to perform a ceremony in which he was facing each of the four directions, I asked him "Why are you doing this here and getting so little sleep? You are a rational man, a Professor at Buffalo University. How can it help you or anyone?"

His reply, as well as I can remember it, was equally direct. "I do it because I must. If those responsible in each region do not perform these ceremonies every day, the connection between our world and the higher world will be broken and the higher energies will not reach our land, the climate will be disrupted, the rains will not come, life will not produce our children and our crops, and violence will spread in all directions. That is my function, my service."

From my own experience I believe it is true that the vivifying energies from above can only reach our planet through human beings when they are awake. Sleeping people are not conscious enough to receive these finer energies.

In the Kabbalah also it is stated that for the earth to survive there must at all times be thirty-six "righteous persons" living and practicing this transmission. Today is a very difficult time, so no doubt we need more than thirty-six at present. Gurdjieff told Ouspensky that he thought "two hundred *conscious people,* if they existed, and if they found it necessary and legitimate, could change the whole of life on the earth." Surely it does not matter from which tradition or spiritual teaching these conscious people come. It only matters that they have reached the level of awakening and are not just deluding themselves and others, as is too often the case these days.

From this perspective, it is not necessarily a matter of "doing" versus "being." More and more people are finding it possible to combine both approaches, using the experiences of daily life as a spiritual discipline, and "walking their talk." Now more than ever, there is a need for an inner work in the midst of ordinary life, a call to awaken and be attentive to an alert awareness that begins—not ends—when we get up from sitting on our cushions.

This 'work on oneself' to be more awake in the midst of one's ordinary life is the hallmark of the Gurdjieff teaching. G.I. Gurdjieff was a Greek-Armenian born in Alexandropol (now Gumri), Russia (now Armenia), probably in 1866. He died in Paris in 1949, almost unknown, but since then he has become recognized as a great contemporary spiritual teacher. His aim, in Jacob Needleman's words, "was to awaken human beings to the meaning of our existence and to the efforts we must make to realize that meaning in the midst of the life that we have been given." If you wish to know more about Gurdjieff and his famous pupil, P.D. Ouspensky, read their books. (See Recommended Reading.) Some years ago, in *Asking for the Earth,* I wrote extensively about Gurdjieff and his teaching. I also recommend that you read the Introduction to Dr. Needleman's more recently published *The Inner Journey: Views from the Gurdjieff Work.*

Governments talk "green" but act only when public opinion forces them to do so. We need to build a global coalition on a scale and at a speed never before attempted. Gordon Brown, on his first visit to the United Nations as Britain's Prime Minister, on July 31, 2007, called for a "coalition of conscience." Nothing less, it seems to me, is going to bring China, India, and the developing world into a deal with the G8 developed countries that ensures that obligations to reduce greenhouse gas emissions are shared fairly and globally. Such a coalition can and should begin with the integration of the environmental and spiritual movements in the Western countries, which have been the biggest polluters. From these strategic beginnings, we can hope that the changes we are trying to bring about will quickly spread and be empowered by a force far larger and stronger than we are—the force of life itself.

Business talks "green," and a few (often those that have enlightened CEOs) are green. But the priority for most businesses is to make money. While some sell new green products, most of them are still resisting carbon taxation and the ecological tax incentives needed initially to subsidize beneficial new technologies.

In the meantime, while governments and businesses dither, Nature is having to turn up the heat on us, in a conjunction of ozone layer depletion, carbon emissions destabilizing global climate, earthquakes and hurricanes increasing in frequency and intensity, coral reefs dying, tropical forests disappearing, and fertile areas becoming deserts. It is the conjunction of all these events that raises a real question as to how long humanity can survive the consequences of its maltreatment of Nature. She is turning up the heat both physically and psychologically, in what seems to me a last-ditch effort to get humanity to wake up, to enlarge our picture of reality and to begin behaving, not as dysfunctional predators but as responsible stewards of the planet. If we had not been so deeply asleep, we might have listened to our scientists sooner; we might have learned our lesson before Nature had to invoke the ultimate threat of our very survival. Now, as slow learners, we are confronted by the dire alternative: change or perish. Perhaps Nature has, by now, no other choice. "If they don't wake up with a gentle tap, try slapping them harder and harder until they do!" The sooner we respond, the better it will be for us and for our descendants.

When I open my eyes, my view of reality is enlarged. I see more of the whole; the more I see, the more I become aware that what I had thought of as the whole is not everything that is. When I was young, the best astrophysicists thought they knew that our galaxy was the entire Universe. Now they know that there are billions of galaxies. What else still lies beyond our scientific ken, beyond what we now take to be everything?

And that is only the outward perspective. How little we have studied the inner world of consciousness scientifically! No wonder the cognitive sciences are exploding with new discoveries in this long neglected domain. Is inner space the last frontier or are there others to be uncovered as our view of wholeness expands? Physics is exploring new dimensions, but the other sciences have been slow to accept the hypothesis that reality may be multileveled and that some levels may be off-limits to our puny faculties of knowing. For human cognition, everything may be much less than All. Indeed, what we think we know, at this early point in our evolution, may turn out to be an obstacle to our developing a better understanding of the Whole. A more open attitude of *not knowing* is more likely to take us deeper into the mystery of the Unknown, because it frees our attention to move in new directions, unimpeded by our habitual identification with old modes of thinking that have outlived their usefulness.

It is, I think, remarkable that it has taken so long—a century at least—for the idea of the interconnectedness of everything to penetrate into our Western culture. We still think that we are separate skin-encapsulated individuals, existing independently of one another in a world of objects, whereas, according to quantum mechanics, our bodies, and all the so-called objects that we see around us, are really more like patterns of energy relationships than solid things. And so this old way of thinking in which we are stuck prevents us from grasping the reality of distant viewing or healing, and many other aspects of non-local paranormal phenomena, which are still being dismissed as unreal because our old scientific paradigm has no explanation for them.

I see now that the world I thought of as real even ten years ago is no more than one of the outer veils of that Greatness that is the Source of all forms of what we casually call life. Indeed, I can no longer assume that I at last begin to understand reality, since my understanding has undergone so many changes during ninety years. Equally important, I see that these changes are actually accelerating, and that these changes are happening not only to me but to a number of my friends. So I suspect that something is shifting in the consciousness of humans on this planet, and evolving faster and faster, as what we call time goes by.

Nothing happens without a reason in a lawful universe, and the reason for this change in human consciousness is already blatantly obvious: the old consciousness that was sufficient for us in the primitive stages of our history has now become a danger to all life on this poor planet. Without a very rapid change of behavior, we will spoil the ecological systems on which life depends. There can be no change in our behavior without a change in our consciousness. If that is what Nature needs, it should not surprise us that this is what is happening. Nature has a good track record for getting what she wants—one way or another—and she no longer needs the old "survival of the fittest" human consciousness. It is incompatible with our present technological prowess and the present need to cooperate for common goals. Mature technology requires an awakened conscience; without it, humans become a danger to themselves and to all forms of life. Objectively speaking, unless they can shape up to the requirements of life, they deserve to be discarded.

Thanks to Nature turning up the heat, we are beginning to understand that humanity needs to take a radically new direction, to be actively aware of our relationship with the earth, with all the other species of life, with each other and with ourselves. We need to awaken to each of these relationships, for they are all interacting with each other in the dynamic of the whole. Nothing is separate.

When I see my situation, when I wish to awaken and wonder how to go about it, I can begin with what is closest to me and most practical: myself. *I can begin in stillness, simply by bringing my attention down from my head and into my body, relaxing its tensions, until, if I persist, I have the beginning of an awareness of being present here now, at this moment.* Sometimes this practice is called *remembering myself,* sometimes *prayer.* As all the sages of all the ages affirm, that is the first step on the way to an awakening of consciousness. All it takes is a small shift of my attention from outer to inner, from my thoughts to the physical awareness of my alive body. Almost immediately I may feel life circulating wherever I pay attention, in every part of my body. At the same time, with practice, I can be aware of everything happening around me. I can be present, awake.

But then what happens? Almost always, I find that this great feeling of waking up, of freedom and aliveness, vanishes so quickly that I hardly know it happened. Then I find myself back in my head thinking about it, worrying about it, devoid of sensations below the neck and with only a vague memory of presence, its immediacy forgotten. That is what I mean by sleep.

Only when we are truly awake can we play our role as human beings in the cosmic dance of life. Thinking about it, worrying about it, won't do it. Instead we need to get good at it—and soon. This inner practice can bring about the sort of transformation of human consciousness that is needed to change our behavior, give birth to a new Renaissance, and save our planetary home from burning.

CHAPTER 3

Called to Awaken But Still Asleep

Sleeping people live each in their own world; only
those who are awake have a world in common.

HERACLITUS

A few months ago, my wife and I decided that we really
must give up the convenience of bringing home our daily
food shopping in plastic bags. Toronto has had to export its
garbage across the border to Michigan and Michigan does not
want it any more. Nobody does. Plastic bags last forever and
are definitely unfriendly to the environment. So we decided we
would not use them. But the next time we went grocery shopping, we forgot to bring the cloth bags we had bought and had
to come home with plastic. And the next time. And …

It took us weeks to break the habit and form a new one. Our
minds had decided but our bodies were wired to the plastic bag
habit, and we had to work on our forgetting before a new habit
could be established. In the process, we had the opportunity
to see how mechanical our habits are and what a strong force
maintains our mechanical behavior—the same blind behavior
that on the global scale is now threatening to undermine the
earth's life-support systems. We had a chance to study our sleep
and what a determined effort is needed to change or wake up.
We had to remember not just the cloth shopping bags; we had

to remember ourselves and work on ourselves, with our minds, through our feelings for the planet and in our lazy bodies. Only when they came together did we change.

And so it is in a myriad of ways in our daily lives. We think we are awake and fail to see how everything happens by itself, while we identify with our distracting dreams instead of paying attention. This inability to see our actual situation reinforces our hypnotic sleep—and our collective failure to see in good time that humanity is destroying the environment on which we all depend. That is just another example of what I am calling sleep.

This may also help to clarify what I mean by "awakening." Sometimes a personal shock is necessary to wake up, and sometimes it takes the big eco-shocks of climate change to do the trick. But to stay awake we must *intend* to remain aware in this more alive way, which is as dramatic a change of state as ordinary awakening is when compared to ordinary sleep. And that intention to stay awake is only fed by seeing, time and again, what we are up against: a force that resists our awakening and reinforces our automatic mechanical actions and reactions. Until we have seen that in ourselves—as when we tried to switch from plastic bags to cloth shopping bags—and seen it repeatedly, we blithely assume that we are awake already and no more demanding efforts are required of us to awaken.

Ever since humans began to reflect on the forces shaping our destiny on this planet, our sages and prophets have tried to be in dialogue with the presumed Creator of these forces in order that they and their "tribes" could live in harmony with the Creator. In one form or another the sages and prophets were asking the question that should resonate today as never before: "What can we do, or be, to serve You?"

At different times, and still today, a few real pioneers of humanity have addressed such questions to God, or to the Universe, Nature, the Cosmos, Consciousness or the Akashic Field. I am neither a sage nor a prophet, but I would address this question to the Unknown, which for me is not limited to any designation by a human mind. This word, the Unknown, evokes in me a deep feeling of awe for an omnipresent field of cosmic energy—the energy of life, intelligent energy, compassionate energy, wholeness. In asking such a question, I would try at every moment to remember that I am asking the Unknown to give me intimations of what, in my ordinary state of consciousness, may be unknowable. So "Lord, have mercy," along with a deep wish for awakening, is the only appropriate attitude.

Is that a futile pursuit? Am I fooling myself in hoping for any kind of objective response? If I think I can receive on demand an answer by my own efforts, I probably am. But if I feel in my gut that the Unknown wants to communicate with humans and the only obstacle is that we are not paying attention, then I have an obligation—even a sacred obligation—to listen intently for the "whispers from the other shore," and to listen as often as I am able to be present, open, and receptive to these higher vibrations. I cannot, on my own initiative, make contact with the higher, but I do not want to be asleep when I am being called from above to awaken. After all, if you were running the whole show, wouldn't you want to get those errant human beings on Planet Earth to smarten up and change their stupidly unsustainable ways? Wouldn't you be trying to wake them up before they spoil your Work—this beautiful blue planet hanging in space? If we are, as all traditions maintain, made in God's image, surely this is a legitimate inference for us to make.

This approach does have its risks. It is subjective. We are very far from running the show and our speculations must suffer from an anthropomorphic bias. They can go off track, lured by some wild imagination triggered not from above but from below, from my illusion of self-importance and my grandiloquent assumption that I really know. I must not forget my need to verify everything as rigorously as I can, to the extent that this is possible. At the same time, I must not forget to trust the promptings of conscience and genuine intuition, which can so easily give up when confronted by my critical mind alone.

So, with these cautions, let us try to ask the question of how to serve, not just intellectually, but with our whole being—mind, feeling, body, and soul—to ask as if we were asking the Being-of-Beings. Surely it is only when we assume that our own personal being is a particle of that Greatness, just as our life is a part of the great Life, that we may hope for an answer that is not totally subjective but is in some degree (depending on the quality of our wishing) objective. *As above, so below.* If the microcosm is indeed made in the image of the macrocosm, intercommunication must be not a mere human fantasy but an aspect of the interconnectedness that is such a fundamental feature of the whole.

When we begin to feel our connection with the whole, and therefore with each other, as a presence, we are ready to understand what Heraclitus was trying to tell us so long ago:

> Sleeping people live each in their own world; only those who are awake have a world in common.

CHAPTER 4

Framing the Question of Our Survival

We are not going to be able to operate our Spaceship
Earth successfully nor for much longer unless we see
it as a whole spaceship and our fate as common. It
has to be everybody or nobody.

BUCKMINSTER FULLER

A s you can see by now, there are many aspects, many levels, to awakening to the question of our survival. Leaving
aside for the moment the metaphysical ponderings of the last
chapter, the central down-to-earth question for most of humanity at this time is—or ought to be—"How can we survive
climate change in the 21st century?" However, according to the
Pew Research Center, climate change comes in 19th on the list
of major concerns in the United States, the country with the
most responsibility for causing the problem, and 20th in China, the second largest polluter.

On any rational analysis or cold hard look, it seems to me
that, in this century, humanity could (to adapt T.S. Eliot's
lines) go out with a nuclear bang or with the whimper of global
warming, as we rapidly make our hospitable planet inhospi-
table, not only for ourselves but possibly for all life. No wonder
that Lord Rees, Britain's Astronomer Royal and President of
the Royal Society, has been warning all who have ears to hear

that he thinks humanity's chances of making it through this century are no better than fifty-fifty. What a wake up call!

And by no means the first. On November 18, 1992, the Union of Concerned Scientists, acting on behalf of over 1,600 eminent scientists, including a majority of all the living Nobel Laureates in the sciences, issued a *Warning to Humanity*. This is how it begins:

> Human beings and the natural world are on a collision course. Human activities inflict harsh and often irreversible damage on the environment and on critical resources. If not checked, many of our current practices put at serious risk the future that we wish for human society and the plant and animal kingdoms, and may so alter the living world that it will be unable to sustain life in the manner that we know. Fundamental changes are urgent if we are to avoid the collision our present course will bring about.

The warning then goes on to deal specifically with the "*critical stress*" suffered by the atmosphere, water resources, oceans, soil, forests, living species and "*the pressures of unrestrained (human) population growth.*" It concludes:

> A great change in our stewardship of the earth and the life on it is required, if vast human misery is to be avoided and our global home on this planet is not to be irretrievably mutilated.

Finally, it goes on to say what we must do to change our behavior, listing changes that fifteen years later are still on humanity's to do list.

The Global Footprint Network has been keeping track of the impact humanity—all 6.6 billion of us—is having on the earth. Since the 1980s, we have been taking more than our planet can renew, and are now recklessly extracting 25% more than is sustainable. In 40 years there will likely be 9 billion of us, for, although our rate of population growth is slowing, we are still growing by 80 million people a year. Something has to change to stabilize our numbers and reduce our demands on the environment on which we all depend. And at last many of us are becoming aware of the danger we face.

On July 7, 2007, the Live Earth concerts and Al Gore's message were heard by about two billion people. Millions responded with pledges to do something specific about reducing their carbon footprints and getting their governments into action to stop or moderate the effects of climate change on us. In his email on the day after the event, this is what Mr. Gore wrote:

> All of the actions we take from here on out to solve the climate crisis will be based on a simple premise: our home, Earth, is in danger. We don't risk destroying the planet, but instead risk making it inhospitable for human beings.

> We have put so much carbon dioxide into the atmosphere that we have changed the heat balance between Earth and the Sun. If we don't stop soon, the average temperature will increase to levels that will end the favorable climate balance on which our civilization depends.

Throughout most of our short history, the United States and the American people have provided moral leadership for the world. Establishing the Bill of Rights, framing democracy in the Constitution, defeating Fascism in World War II, toppling Communism, and landing on the moon—all were the result of American leadership.

Once again, Americans must come together and direct our government to take on a global challenge. Our leadership is a precondition for success.

We need to demonstrate that we have reached the tipping point where political will demands our representatives take action to solve the climate crisis.

The climate crisis offers us the chance to experience what few generations in history have had the privilege of experiencing: a mission; a compelling moral purpose; a shared cause; and the thrill of being forced by circumstances to put aside the pettiness and conflict of politics and to embrace a genuine moral and spiritual challenge.

Tipping points are easier to see in retrospect than when they are happening. We may not know for another decade whether we are today at a tipping point; but already there are some signs of an awakening. In June, 2007, climate change was front and center on the G8 nations meeting of Presidents and Prime Ministers of the most (economically) developed countries. Once again they failed to agree on what to do about it. Indeed, I believe we are all failing to acknowledge the magnitude of the danger we are facing and the magnitude of the changes *in us* that are going to be necessary to overcome it. Without major changes in how humanity is behaving in polluting the environment, I cannot see how even the most hopeful scenario of technological improvements and stringent governmental regulations worldwide is going to make enough difference. Can we alter the growing momentum of the convergence of life-threatening climate changes? Not, I would say, without changing ourselves in the process.

As Pogo, the comic strip character from the 1940s, said, "We have met the enemy and he is us." We need to learn how to change not just the system, but our greedy consumerism—ourselves—cell by cell and habit by habit. To survive, we need without question to awaken. And the timeline by which this must happen is shrinking year by year with each new and more comprehensive scientific model. The best scientific predictions of a few years ago gave us a few generations. Now they give us a few decades at best, perhaps only a few years. The shock of the rapidity of the climate crisis, especially at the North and South Poles, is forcing all of us to take stock of the fact that we are much deeper into the ecological crisis, much sooner than we thought even a few years ago. Now, nothing less than a basic change in human behavior will suffice. It is in truth, as Al Gore said, "a genuine moral and spiritual challenge" of daunting proportions. Nothing less than a change of being in a critical mass of humanity will change the present negative human impact on our planet.

Have we the courage, individually and collectively, to face that requirement? I am not sure we have. Do we look with paralyzing fear at the prospect of a dead earth? We need first to look with love at our incredibly beautiful planet as seen from space—a space that invokes in all of us, as we gaze up at the stars on a dark night, a sense that there is a benevolent intelligence behind and within Creation, and within our deepest self. That sense of oneness with the Universe, no separation, is really a feeling of love. With that love there comes an inner confidence—almost a certainty—that if we do our part, the Universe is not about to write off Planet Earth. That is how I answer the question for myself, as honestly as I can. As Michael Shellenberger has said, "Martin Luther King didn't give an 'I have a nightmare' speech; he gave an 'I have a dream' speech." Love always trumps fear.

We are being tested rigorously, but I believe that the conditions for our awakening are at hand, and that we will make it, as we always have, when we have to. It will be break through—not break down. Four billion years of evolution is not about to go down the tube on this planet. There must be and there will be a new Renaissance in the 21st century, and we who are alive today have both the blessing and the curse of living at this crucial cosmic tipping point. Let us face this challenge from our love for the earth and therefore from our wish to save it—not from our fear of global warming. Fearing global warming is just another form of our fear for our recalcitrant self-serving selves. As Jesus told us, "perfect love casts out fear." The opposite is also true: perfect (or imperfect) fear casts out love.

CHAPTER 5

The Ecological Crisis Is Fundamentally a Spiritual Crisis

> O Lord God and all your helpers, help me to remember myself, always and everywhere, so that less evil may enter Thy creation.
>
> G.I. GURDJIEFF, *The Struggle of the Magicians*

In the mid 1960s, when I was the Minister (or Deputy Ambassador) at the Canadian Embassy in Paris, I knew André Malraux, who was Minister of Culture in General de Gaulle's government. No one would have thought of him as a spiritual pioneer, but towards the end of his life two decades later, this great agnostic intellectual surprised everyone by proclaiming: "Our century has rediscovered, through psychoanalysis, the demons in man; the 21st century will be a spiritual century, or it will not be at all."

At the time, I thought he was being his provocative self; he loved to shock. Today, it seems to me more likely that he was foreseeing, with the clarity sometimes preceding death, where the shallowness of contemporary Western culture was leading us, and warning us of the urgent need to change course or reap the whirlwind.

As I see it now, humanity has, especially in the past century, developed an addiction to consuming much more than it needs. This addiction has been fostered by those who have an interest in keeping the global markets growing at any cost—in human misery, ecological destruction and unsustainable resource depletion—all for the benefit of multi-national corporations which are, with few exceptions, intent on maximizing profits regardless of the consequences for the environment. To this end, corporations and the advertisers who sell their products have made use of the discoveries of Freud and Jung, and the timely arrival of television as a marketing tool, to condition the mass of humanity to be addicted to consumption. And, as with all addictions, we, the addicted, are oblivious (or asleep) to our condition, in denial when it is pointed out, maintaining that we are not in the least addicted and there is no problem. Only when we begin to open our eyes and awaken to our actual crisis can we hope to break free of our addiction.

The good news is that we now know that it is "not in our stars," and it is not because of our genetic makeup that we are addicted. We can choose to break the habit. Neuroscientists have discovered in the past few years that the hardware of the brain is not fixed and immutable, but extraordinarily adaptable. They are now calling this the neuroplasticity of the brain: everything we think and do with attention changes the circuitry of the brain. That means we can change our behavior if we really wish. We need not accept our addictions, manipulated by powerful vested interests, as the norm for human beings. Operating largely under the radar of public awareness and outside government control, these international corporations are playing the game of making money on a global scale. But some corporations are beginning to see that it is not in their long term interests to behave so irresponsibly. They are going to sink with the rest of us, if the whole ship goes down.

If the good news is that the brain is adaptable, the bad news is that addictive behavior is hard to stop. As the founders of Alcoholics Anonymous discovered long ago, my first step in stopping any addiction is to acknowledge that I have a problem. It's easy to see in others, but my inner defense mechanisms interpret it as a threat to my identity or self-image and conceal it from my conscious awareness. Sometimes a big shock is needed to jolt me awake. Maybe something like that is what we are getting these days. We are being jolted globally by the "war on terror," and in our own families by the "war on drugs," on top of the nuclear nightmare we thought had gone away with the end of the cold war and the global warming we have been denying for thirty years with gradually decreasing conviction.

After the accumulated shocks have awakened my attention and I begin to perceive that I do have a problem, the next layer of denial pretends that the problem is really quite superficial— nothing serious. I can resolve it by a few easy half-measures, which I plan to get around to when I can—but always later. The great spiritual master of the last century, G.I. Gurdjieff, called it "the disease of tomorrow." And so I change too little and too late, until I am literally out of time.

That scenario, it seems to me, is frighteningly apt today. Collectively, we are belatedly beginning to wake up in response to the loss of so many species and so many major dislocations in the ecological systems that sustain life. The losses are so significant that we can only ignore them at our own peril. We are not going to escape from the worst consequences of global warming simply by changing light bulbs, recycling a little, and developing new (and of course profitable) technologies that will resolve the problem the same way we are told that we have resolved (I wish it were true!) the ozone layer erosion problem by giving up the use of chlorofluorocarbons (CFCs) in the Montreal Protocol of 1989.

The most "inconvenient truth," is that we are going to have to give up a lifestyle that requires us to consume growing quantities of finite non-renewable resources to the point that there soon won't be enough left to sustain our addiction. In decades, we have used up what Nature spent millions of years laying down. No new technological fix will make that fact go away. And our mushrooming population, approaching seven billion, will ensure that, whatever new energy technologies are developed, the growth of demand will continue to outstrip the supply of non-renewable resources. Gandhi put it more simply: "There is enough for everyone's need, but not for anyone's greed."

So can we give up our habitual greediness? Can we make that big a change in behavior patterns that threaten to endanger our species and perhaps the whole of life on this planet? And can we do it not in a thousand years but in one generation? After that, it may well be too late to stabilize our climate or reverse its degradation enough to sustain most forms of life, including our own.

With the shock of Pearl Harbor in 1941, America managed in a few months to transform its capacity to make cars into a capacity to make planes and tanks, and then the atom bomb. The Manhattan Project of the 21st century must be a spiritual—not just a technological—project: the rapid evolution of the real human being to its full potential.

In all traditions, human beings have been seen as having a cosmic function—a link between Earth and Heaven, allowing energies that are higher in vibration and finer in quality to reach our planet, in this remote corner of the Universe, through our bodies. That, I presume, is what we were designed for—why we are here. Nothing else will do it. Yes, humanity is in its infancy, not having quite learned the quality of self awareness that is necessary for us to do this. Yet, perhaps this is the time when we must learn how to fulfill that function, or perish—a failed experiment that fouled its own nest irretrievably and never got past toilet training. After putting up with a great deal of abuse from us for a very long time, it would not be surprising if Nature's patience were nearly exhausted. Nature needs a new humanity at this time, and it will either get it—by humanity evolving to fulfill its function—or, if we fail to evolve, by getting us out of the way, as has happened to other species that have disappeared. The stakes are, I believe, that awesome, and we don't improve our chances by looking the other way or shrugging helplessly.

As we face up to our prospective future and let this realization that we must change ourselves sink in to our conscience, must we not conclude that the outcome may depend on how many of us, and how soon, accept this view? Can we see our perilous predicament and really begin to take it seriously, act on it, live it, suffer it, moment by moment? Could this be part of the cosmic game plan at this time? Yes, we tend to dismiss grandiose talk about cosmic game plans with our critical minds. It is indeed far beyond our means of knowing. But what if it is true, as many teachings say? If so, could it not help to energize us over the huge hurdle of change that we are facing? At least we know that the hurdle is real and that, if we are to overcome it in time, we must grasp at whatever psychological props may help us, whether or not we can prove to ourselves in advance the truth or falsity of the prop. For we are in desperate times and no longer have the luxury of being able to verify everything before trying it. The experiment will either verify or disprove the attempt. What have we got to gain by holding back, when we have everything to lose by our habitual skeptical passivity? That is just another form of our collective addiction, our denial, our sleep.

The ecological crisis is fundamentally a spiritual crisis. In his 1992 best seller, *Earth in the Balance: Ecology and the Human Spirit,* Al Gore said it beautifully:

> The more deeply I search for the roots of the global environmental crisis, the more I am convinced that it is an outer manifestation of an inner crisis that is, for lack of a better word, spiritual.

As leaders in the churches and mosques and synagogues and zendos and temples come to realize that we are in a spiritual-ecological crisis and see the urgency of action, things can change rapidly. To take just one example, the Catholic Church, with about a billion followers: Pope John Paul II gave the lead in his New Year's Day message of 1990—seven years before the

Kyoto protocol—when he spoke feelingly of the "suffering" of the planet from "environmental degradation," and foresaw "the threat of ecological breakdown" caused by our culture of "instant gratification and consumerism" and "vastly increased energy needs." Under Pope Benedict, the Vatican recently set out to become the first carbon-neutral state in the world, although it may take more than 1,000 solar panels on Vatican rooftops to accomplish that great objective. That influence moves quickly. In September, 2007, I saw a huge array of solar panels covering the Bavarian countryside near Munich and solar panels on many church roofs in Sibiu, Romania—and not only on Catholic churches. At least in Europe, it's catching on! But what about the USA and Canada, to say nothing of China and India?

If we are to make it through the 21st century, our ecologically destructive human behavior must stop. New creative technologies and wise government regulations strictly enforced will help, but it is my contention that nothing less than a change of consciousness in humanity as a whole, starting with you and with me right now, is needed. Thanks to the timely discoveries of the neuroscientists, we know that the brain can adapt to change and that a change of consciousness is indeed possible.

What sort of change is a shift in consciousness? If I see that we need to evolve as a species, where do I, as an individual, begin? How do I become a truly human being? What am I to do or to be? For what purpose was I born? And then, waiting for our best attention, is the question behind all questions: *who am I?*

CHAPTER 6

The Next Step in Human Evolution

In speaking of evolution it is necessary to understand from the outset that no mechanical evolution
is possible. The evolution of man is the evolution of
his consciousness. *And "consciousness" cannot evolve
unconsciously.* The evolution of man is the evolution
of his will, and "will" cannot evolve involuntarily.
The evolution of man is the evolution of his power
of doing, and "doing" cannot be the result of things
which "happen."

G.I. GURDJIEFF, as quoted by P.D. Ouspensky,
In Search of the Miraculous

We know how to change the oil in our car; but we don't
understand what a change of consciousness would en-
tail—still less how to bring it about. But if we can now see that
such a change is required for our survival, it is surely time to
start addressing the issue and looking for help wherever we can
find it.

My starting point is the proposition that human consciousness can evolve. In fact, it has been doing so all along, in parallel
with our emergence from the water to the land, and then from
the forest to the savannah, from hunting/gathering to farm-
ing and villages, from the industrial revolution to the Internet

revolution. I am not arguing that changes in technology have led to changes in consciousness, although they do often seem to have gone hand-in-hand. Through all these transitions, we now know that we have been constantly changing our brains by how we behave, what we do, and how we think.

In the course of these evolutionary interactions, there have been a few times when there have been sudden leaps forward. One such period was in the 6th and 5th centuries B.C. when such great figures as Lao Tzu, Confucius, Zoroaster, the Buddha, and Socrates initiated new directions within their respective cultural frameworks. So too did Moses, Christ, and Mohammed at other points in time. The Renaissance—with Dante, Leonardo de Vinci, and Galileo—was another, so different from the past that it seemed like a new birth for humanity. It is too early to see our own times clearly but my guess is that today we are well into another such formative period, when old paradigms give way almost overnight to new ways of seeing and knowing the world and ourselves. In each case, it is as if our planet is being fed new ideas when they are needed to ensure that changes in both the outlook and the "inlook" that determine our behavior take place on cue, as required not merely for human but for larger, even cosmic, purposes.

The great spiritual revolutionaries of history could then be seen as the vehicles through whom the energies of these living ideas are transmitted to humanity, as seeds of change, of growth, and of life. Yet, after each burst of creativity changes the human landscape for a while, the revolution is betrayed and the human horizon contracts again, so that less light can enter. Still, some small communities always manage to keep alive for future generations the understanding that has been gained, and from these holy communities the next pioneer spiritual leaders can arise, as needed.

The lesson we still need to learn from the great Masters of all the traditions is that they did not come to serve as objects of devotion, but as exemplars of what we are designed to become—if we awaken. For, as Gurdjieff put it, "if one man (or woman) can, anyone can." The Masters show us the real nature of the human potential, what it means to BE a real man or a woman, not (as Gurdjieff wrote) a "man" (or "woman") in quotation marks. And you and I, in turn, can feel the spur of remorse for how far we are from realizing what the great Teachers showed us to be humanly possible.

In the past five years, the next step in human evolution has become both more practical and more possible. As has already been mentioned, American cognitive scientists, working in collaboration with the Dalai Lama and some of his meditation masters, have brought us the good news that our brains are not static, not fixed for life with a genetically determined set of neurons, decaying as we age, but are malleable and adaptable throughout life, capable of growing new neurons and interconnections as we think new thoughts and practice new skills. This ground-breaking research, chiefly in the laboratory of Dr. Richard Davidson of the University of Wisconsin in Madison, has shown that this neuroplasticity of the brain depends on a certain quality of attention that can be developed by rigorous meditative practices and intensive skills, such as those displayed by a trained pianist or dancer, for example. In these ways, with attention, we can train our minds, and even our bodies, to change our brains. And a changed brain does not think or behave in the ways the old brain behaved. It is now becoming established that this is verifiably possible. You can read more about this in the recent books of the Dalai Lama, Daniel Goleman, Alan Wallace, and Sharon Begley, and on the website of the Mind and Life Institute founded by Adam Engle.

Not to be outdone by the cognitive scientists, a new generation of biologists has been creating what might be considered a new biology, epigenetics. Epi- means "above" or "in addition to" and, in the past decade, this newcomer has, along with neuroplasticity studies, begun to free us from the confines of genetic determinism. In *The Biology of Belief,* Bruce Lipton draws a sharp contrast between the old and the new biology:

> A world defined by neo-Darwinism casts life as an unending war among battling, biochemical robots. On the other side ... the "New Biology" casts life as a cooperative journey among powerful individuals who can program themselves to create joy-filled lives. When we ... truly understand the New Biology, we will no longer fractiously debate the role of nurture and nature, because we will realize that the fully conscious mind trumps both nurture and nature. And I believe we will also experience as profound a paradigmatic change to humanity as when a round-world reality was introduced to a flat-world civilization.

Once we realize that radical and rapid change is indeed possible for human beings, the most important question is how to make the optimum changes as quickly as possible in order to adjust human behavior to the requirements of the planet. In the Buddhist terminology of Tibet, what are the most skillful means to this end? As the Dalai Lama has said, we need to look in all the wisdom traditions and spiritual teachings to see, through objective scientific testing, what works best in this great work of awakening conscience and changing consciousness.

Unfortunately, other traditional teachings and teachers have been much less forthcoming than the Dalai Lama in opening their secrets of inner work and the development of attention to objective study and scientific evaluation. Let us hope that the recent discoveries in the cognitive sciences outlined previously will encourage others to join in the common search for whatever works. If they do not, I expect that they will lose followers to Tibetan Buddhism, whose adepts have astonished the scientists who tested them. Of course, this is not some competitive sideshow to promote one point of view. This is a call for deep trust and cooperation among all religious and spiritual lineages in facing a common emergency for the whole of humanity. We need to face it together.

Perhaps another summit meeting under the auspices of the United Nations Secretary General is needed now, but this time with environmental and spiritual leaders working together on both the consequences and the underlying causes of our destructive human behavior. The spiritual summit in 2001 (which I attended in New York) was held before we knew what we know now about the neuroplasticity of the brain and before the awareness of the urgency of global warming had made almost everyone "green," at least in theory.

The next step towards a truly global coalition is to build a broad strategic alliance between the greens and the spiritual teachings. This will call for strong leadership in both camps to overcome the distaste secular greens have for spiritual progressives, and vice versa. But only when both camps come to realize the necessity of building such a holistic alliance will the combined movement develop the global momentum that is a precondition of success. The crisis we are facing demands nothing less than a truly global response. In Western countries, the secular élites may predominate, but in much of the rest of the world they are obviously not in the ascendant. Those who planned the Iraq and Afghanistan wars should by now have learned that lesson.

In the meantime, what skillful means can already be identified to put us on a more sustainable course towards the greening, not only of our minds, but of the collective actions that are threatening to devastate our Spaceship Earth?

CHAPTER 7

Where Have We Buried Conscience?

To meet the challenge of our times, human beings
will have to develop a greater sense of universal responsibility. Each one of us must learn to work not
just for his, or her, own self, family or nation, but for
the benefit of all mankind.

H.H. THE DALAI LAMA, 2007

In the current secular atmosphere, moral imperatives are out
of fashion; *should* is passé; faith, hope, and love are words
that have lost their deep meaning through overuse; and if conscience still exists and is not simply obsolete, it must be hiding
somewhere, perhaps, as Gurdjieff suggests, in the subconscious.
"May it rest there in peace and not disturb me." So, unfortunately, say most of us sleepers.

Where, then, to begin the process of awakening? The idea
of awakening is interesting. However, without the power of
feeling behind the idea, I don't even rub my sleepy eyes. For
my attention to be effectively engaged, mind, body, and feeling
must participate, and for this to happen a shock or shocks are
almost always needed. Getting a sudden diagnosis of advanced
cancer, or some other threat of imminent death, may do it.
Reading about the possible death of our species, long after my
own demise, may not.

If my grandchildren complain about the ecological debts my generation is about to leave hanging around their necks, I may justify myself by claiming that I did what I could—no one was listening—but soon I will be uneasy, knowing in my heart that I could have done much more to wake myself and others. My conscience is not clear, and feeling the pain for what lies ahead for my grandchildren can bring tears of remorse to my eyes.

If you too are feeling something like that, we can share a common search to awaken. We see and feel the need for it. But if you were to ask me for a recipe for how to do it—just give me ten quick tips for transformation—I could not respond. What works for me may not work for you. Each of us is unique and no one shoe fits all. Each of us must study ourselves and find our own path.

At the same time, none of us can get very far alone. We need individual help from someone with more experience, and we also need the support and interaction of a group of people who are similarly oriented. If you are serious (and not simply shopping around as a dilettante), you can save time by giving up now on the illusion that you can go it alone.

So when it comes to speaking about the skillful means of awakening conscience or raising consciousness, I will limit my advice to a few observations based on long experience and refer you to the sources I have found most helpful. In the end, your salvation is your responsibility, as mine is mine.

Waking up is not an idea; it is an experience—and always a surprise! It can only happen when I am fully attentive in all my parts. It can only happen when I am present, now, sensing the aliveness in my body, aware of my thoughts and feelings, suddenly open to the vastness and beauty of all that is, and feeling that I too am part of that greatness. But before I can become aware of that experience, I will have to free my attention from being constantly glued to each passing thought or feeling—or my backache or headache. Like it or not, I will have to see and feel my inability to be present, my lack of attention, the nullity of my being. I will have to learn to suffer consciously from the absence of presence in me, and to stay in front of that fact as long as possible, remembering and returning when I see that I've forgotten time and again, for as long as it takes, perhaps for years. For only in that way can the boundless luminosity of presence penetrate my endless automatic dreaming in the dark.

All authentic spiritual teachings and traditions say the same thing: "Be here now," "the practice of the presence," "Christ in the heart," "unconditional love," "the unity of being." The great Catholic monk and author, Thomas Merton, traveled to India before his untimely death and I helped him to meet with some of the outstanding Tibetan teachers, including the Dalai Lama. He realized then that those with sufficient experience in their respective spiritual practices can recognize the identical experience behind very different verbal formulations, none of which alone can do justice to the vastness revealed in the experience.

Science no longer disagrees. As Frances Moore Lappe has written in *Getting a Grip (2007):*

> "Soft" psychology as well as "hard" neuroscience
> also confirms that we humans come equipped with
> a moral compass—with deep needs and sensibilities

that make us yearn to end the suffering. Yet we deny these feelings every single day at huge cost to our society and to our world.

Let me elaborate on what I offered in Chapter 1 of this book as a contemporary summation of ancient wisdom. *Begin simply by intentionally relaxing, by bringing the attention to the sensation of life in your body and to the awareness of being present here now, at this moment. Then stay in that state of presence undistracted, if you are able, for one minute.*

I hope you are trying it. That could be your first real step towards self remembering, or the Way, or I AM, or Consciousness. It could be for you, as it has been for me and for many others, the beginning of allowing Presence to become your teacher, regardless of which spiritual tradition you come from, or what you choose to call that empowering force, so needed on this earth at this time.

If you want to go further in the practice of presence and towards awakening, then I recommend that you get in touch with whichever authentic spiritual teaching, ancient or modern, appeals to you and find out, through following their practices, whether it is right for you now. What has helped me most throughout my life is the Work (as it is called) of G.I. Gurdjieff, whom I regard as the great "awakener" of the 20th century. He calls us to bring together the wisdom of the East and the science of the West, and then search. You can find out more about Gurdjieff and his teaching on the Internet at www.gurdjieff.org or through the websites of one of the Gurdjieff Foundations, which maintain his legacy in the lineage of his direct pupils.

Since we are talking about consciousness, let me share with you Gurdjieff's summation of faith, love, and hope in his amazing book, *Beelzebub's Tales to his Grandson.*

Faith of consciousness is freedom
Faith of feeling is weakness
Faith of body is stupidity.

Love of consciousness evokes the same in response
Love of feeling evokes the opposite
Love of body depends only on type and polarity.

Hope of consciousness is strength
Hope of feeling is slavery
Hope of body is disease.

The Hindu teachings tell us that we are now in the Kaliyuga, the end of time, in which there are no secrets anymore. It's true. Yesterday's most sacred secrets are now on the Internet. There is no respect for what earlier generations considered sacred. And every time we use words to describe an experience of the sacred, we inevitably betray and distort it, bring it down to our level—as I have too. That has been true from the beginning. "The way that can be called a way is not the Way." The word that can be called the word is not the Word.

But if we are at the bottom end of time and Truth has been too often betrayed to guide us, how can we face the enormity of what now has to be done in order to survive? If I were to make a judgment with my ordinary mind, I would have to say that humanity is done for—that the challenge we face is more than we can possibly do in the shrinking time remaining for effective action. This despair is demoralizing and paralyzing, reducing our chances still further. And then…?

Then, I remember when I was driving on the highway to Ottawa one snowy night many years ago and suddenly found myself skidding to my death. Something instantly changed: there was no more fear, there was plenty of time to avoid the truck, I was acting appropriately without tension, and the danger was miraculously avoided, as if my guardian angel had been at the wheel. I had wakened up in time—wakened up not from ordinary sleep but from the waking sleep of daydreams that fill our heads almost all the time. In no time, easily, just what had to be done was done, without the feeling that I was doing it.

This shift (when I remember it) reminds me of my innate ability to function quite differently when that is necessary for my survival. From all the evidence, this is not just my personal good fortune. It is an ability inherent in all human beings. At moments when we are awake in this way, we seem to be connected to a much greater intelligence, able to function as if time as we know it did not exist, and given a glimpse of another dimension of reality, perhaps a taste of eternity, and with it a beginning of real love.

As I see it, the cosmic role of every authentic spiritual teaching is to enable a critical mass of humanity to live in this awakened state, not just at moments of dire emergency, but potentially for as much as possible of the time they are given to live in human bodies. This would enable energies from higher up the scale of vibrations to reach the earth through such human conduits and at the same time heal both our ailing planet, and these awakened people.

What is new and exciting today, I feel, is that we have a real cosmic imperative to wake up, not merely for the sake of personal development but as a small individual service towards helping to save our civilization, and perhaps our species, from the ultimate ecological catastrophe. Perhaps soberly but honestly facing that fact will give us the final shock we need to open our selfish hearts. Each of us needs to unbury his or her subconscious conscience, so that it can participate in our actions and modify our life-destructive tendencies. And if that sense of foreboding does not do it, what about love? Let us do everything we can to save the planet simply because we love it.

Do you love our Spaceship Earth and all its wonderful and beautiful forms of life? You would if you had climbed a mountain lately, or been on a canoe trip or a vision quest. If you haven't, go outside and watch the sunrise tomorrow, or at least beg, borrow or rent the BBC's spectacular video series, *Planet Earth*, and let David Attenborough take you around—lovingly.

Now, no more excuses and half-hearted gestures. Prodded by fear and pulled by love, we must give everything we've got— naturally—to save our fragile planetary home!

I hope that you can hear this call to change—to be good stewards of the earth, to be who you are when you can say "I AM," and not feel in your heart that it is a lie.

CHAPTER 8

Are You Called?

Remember God so much that you are forgotten.
Let the caller and the called disappear;
be lost in the call.

JALAL AD-DIN RUMI, *Love is a Stranger*
translated by Kabir Helminski

When I was the Canadian High Commissioner (or Ambassador) in India in the 1960s, one of my friends was Mrs. Welthy Fisher, who founded World Literacy of Canada. She was the widow of a Methodist Bishop. After her husband died, Welthy had returned to India to consult Gandhi as to what useful service she might give the rest of her life. "Should I begin a movement for village education, especially among women?" she had asked him.

Gandhi's advice was simple and applicable to everyone. He asked her, "Are you called?" Only when she replied that she felt that she was, but did not know if she, a foreign woman in a man's world, could bring it off, did Gandhi offer his now famous statement "It is better to light a candle than curse the darkness." In that spirit she began a basic literacy movement that has long outlived her and is now worldwide. If she had begun from only a good idea, I doubt that her initiative would have born such fruit. She was indeed called. There was more than her own energy behind her, and, by acting on her sense of being called, Welthy was opening herself to a higher energy and allowing it to work through her, and do far more than she alone could ever do.

It is my belief that the call today to clean up our ecological act is coming from the same source that called Gandhi and Welthy Fisher and is now calling Al Gore, and so many others, including you and me. We cannot know the source of this call directly but we can see its effects and feel its action in ourselves. When Shakespeare observes that "there is a tide in the affairs of men" that moves us more profoundly than we move ourselves, moving us the way the moon's gravity pulls the ocean tides. It is the action of a doing beyond our doing.

Many times I have felt vivified when I began doing something that I could see was needed, but that, in my laziness, I did not want to do. This infusion of new energy is always a surprise. It is not something I can create or manipulate in any way. I do not know where it comes from but feel that it must be from higher up the chain of command, "the great Chain of Being" in traditional terminology. Many others I know have had similar experiences. Perhaps you have too?

Synchronicities, as Jung called them, multiply when our lives are more connected with whatever is calling us from above. By aligning our personal energies to a higher purpose, one should not be surprised to discover that there is much more than our puny force to help us. At the same time, we learn the hard way that the least self-congratulation or manipulation will kill this mysterious connection.

I am reminded of Mother Theresa's reaction when she was awarded the Nobel Peace Prize: "We don't do big things—nothing great. We do small things, but with great love."

Nor is it required, in all cases, to do anything. All calls are not alike, nor are all people. Some are called to do, some to be. As I see it, some contemplatives in the various traditions manage, consciously or even unconsciously, through long inner practice, to align their personal energies so as to allow higher energies to pass through their bodies and reach the planet. And there may be others, even less well known and less visible, who have found a way to do this even during an active outer life, using the frictions of daily life as a spiritual discipline, without being totally and repeatedly distracted. That path is surely the most demanding and the most rigorous.

This is what Hubert Benoit, coming from the Zen tradition, wrote about the call in *Material for Thought #11,* published by Far West Press:

> This desire is a *rational* desire, related to the existence in me of a divine Reason; it is a wish for truth, for what is real, the only one of its kind among all my irrational desires. More or less intense, depending on the individual, it is a call from Being. As opposed to the other desires, it increases to the extent it is satisfied; it is unquenchable.

What is this call, this force or tide, that activates us, often subliminally? Within the limitations of the current scientific paradigm, it is hard to find a satisfactory explanation. Surely it is time, as the Dalai Lama has written in *The Universe in a Single Atom,* for science to develop a paradigm that allows for a partnership between objective scientific research that is quantifiable and measurable, and "first person research" based in the inner experiences of many observers of how consciousness acts on us and in us. Until that new paradigm has been accepted in the mainstream, the question remains, and it demands an answer. May it lead us towards a new and more inclusive paradigm, allowing us not only to survive this century, but at the same time to resolve some of the paradoxes blocking progress in both physics and biology for the last quarter of a century. We will come to biology, metaphysics, and physics later; but first let us look for the source of what is calling us where it is traditionally most likely to be found—in the force of life itself, or (to use an overused but still potent word) in love.

CHAPTER 9

Reflections on the Power of Love

The day will come when, after harnessing the ether,
the winds, the tides and gravitation, we shall harness
for God the energies of love. And on that day, for the
second time, man will have discovered fire.

TEILHARD DE CHARDIN, *The Evolution of Chastity*

If we are ever to live fully in the holistic age of Aquarius, we
had better not continue to separate our ideals from our daily
life, the sacred from the secular, the higher from the lower, and
love from sex. It is the separation of nation from nation, race
from race, religion from religion, men from women, and the
left hemisphere of our brain from the right hemisphere, that
has produced a species that is despoiling the planet, hypnotized
by the illusion of separation.

As we awaken to the new world of quantum mechanics
and become aware that we are actually living in a totally interconnected world, we begin to discern the holy process of
the spiritualization of the world. As consciousness penetrates
and informs material reality, we can perhaps intuit the action
of that higher energy I spoke of earlier. We could call it God's
energy—lovers call it the action of Love.

On the personal level, when two human beings are joined in
love (as distinct from simply having sex), they can experience on

the human level the resonance of that divine energy. Without that life-giving, vivifying experience, a man is only half a man and a woman only half a woman. Without love, we are not merely asleep; we are virtually dead. To awaken, we need love.

For most of us, to feel our need for love in this way requires an opening, a change of consciousness, a basic change of attitude. This change is not so different as we might imagine from the change of mind I spoke about in earlier chapters as being necessary in order to modify the sort of human behavior that has so upset Nature. Imprisoned in our old habits of mind, we do not even see the need for change and are prevented from entering into the transcendent oneness of making love. I call it "transcendent" because it goes beyond words, beyond social or economic class, beyond color and race, beyond anything that I can think or feel. It connects us to the Source, to the one ground of Being, to Love itself.

Gurdjieff called love the "foundation of everything." And not only Gurdjieff and his successors—all my teachers: the Dalai Lama, Yogaswami in Sri Lanka, Krishnamurti in India and Switzerland, and Dr. Nurbakhsh in Teheran—all spoke of love not as an abstract "field of being" but as the natural energy of living rightly. Love is not something I do; it is something I am—and I am not the doer, love is.

If we remain enclosed in the old view of separateness, we are almost always impervious to the power of love. In a state of separateness, closed to the higher, even sexual intercourse becomes no more than a fleeting pleasure, far removed from the real ecstasy of oneness. What a waste of the highest energy substance that is produced in the human body!

As I have grown older, I have observed that many of my peers lost the will to live when they lost their partners, or when their partnerships stopped being loving. As people enter their sixties, seventies or eighties, their sex life may diminish but does not need to stop. To keep it alive longer, older people in particular need a change of mind in this domain also—a change in what is considered normal. We need to pay much more attention to our own longings and desires than to what may be considered normal in the media or by our friends and families.

This change could be greatly facilitated by adopting an attitude to sex that is much more prevalent in what Arnold Toynbee used to call "the other half of the world," east of Suez. This tantric attitude includes a wish for union and wholeness, tenderness and joy, while giving up our identification with orgasm as synonymous with sex. Especially as we get older, if we are more restrained, we can use the power of our intention to postpone orgasm or avoid it altogether—saving our precious energy for another night, another day. In this way our pleasure and our life can be extended. That is my experience.

Just as there can be sex without love, there can be love without sex, especially for the elderly. Physical closeness, intimacy, caring words and actions all express the generosity that is fueled by love. For the energy of love is not merely a physical energy, just as the practice of compassion does not require physical passion.

Spinoza has helped us to understand that all happiness and unhappiness depends on the quality of what we love. *Love toward the eternal and infinite ... feeds the mind with a joy entirely exempt from sadness. This is greatly to be desired, and to be sought with all our strength.* ("The Emendation of the Intellect," Bollingen Series, p. 9)

Is this another way of speaking about what Barbara Marx Hubbard calls the "vocational arousal of supra-sexual co-creation"—the fire in the belly that arises when I *know* that I am working for what is needed now, not just for my personal satisfaction but for much greater—perhaps cosmic—purposes?

The power of love changes our consciousness and our conscience. That change then cascades naturally into social change and a change in our attitude to the earth. As the great Vietnamese Buddhist monk, Thich Nhat Hanh, has put it, "*Out of love and the willingness to act selflessly, strategies, tactics, and techniques for social change will arise naturally.*"

"Make Love—not War!" is a slogan from the Vietnam war era, but the apposition of love and violence is still directly meaningful today, as the Iraq and Afghanistan wars continue abroad and as our culture of violence continues to dominate television screens at home. Never has it been more apparent that, in almost all our relationships—with the Highest, with Nature, among nations, within each country, city, and family, and with ourselves—there is a terrifying lack of love. The earth would not be burning if it were otherwise. We need love as we need air.

Whether or not we think of the earth as Gaia, a goddess, or in more secular terms, she (or it) needs our love. We cannot measure it yet as we do carbon dioxide, but one day we may be able to assess how much love is in the atmosphere of our planet, the way we now measure the intensity of ultraviolet or carbon dioxide. It is as if the air around this planet has too few parts-per-million of love in it now and destructive human behavior is mirroring that lack—or is this perspective our way of blaming "circumstances" as a convenient alternative to seeing our own failures to love? In any case, we need to change, not merely what we do but what we are: to change our consciousness. We no longer have a choice. If we wish to survive, we have to change. This means letting love into our hearts, our minds, and our bodies. That is the meaning of *ahimsa* or non-violence. Far from being passive, it is a virile action, the action of the highest force in the universe that we are capable of receiving and embodying.

It's more than changing our minds. It's shifting from a love of power to the power of love as one's motivating source. It's changing who I am, cell by cell. Are you ready to practice love, embody love, radiate love—moment by moment, unconditionally, towards your partner, your family, yourself, and toward *all* your neighbors, day after day, and year after year? None of us can honestly say that we can do this, but all of us can be empowered to try more often when we allow ourselves to remember what is really at stake in this great crisis of our time on earth.

Prose is not the language of love, so let me conclude this chapter with a poem I wrote about love—or the lack of it.

Without love, even the song birds are silent,
So should I be surprised that my life is a sleep and a
    forgetting
Without love?

And not only for me; every society and the earth itself,
Bound by the same laws as we are, will collapse and die
Without love!

To get this far towards an awakening of the human has
    taken
Maybe fifteen billion years of Conscious loving.
Are we going to let it all go,
Without love?

What use is all our knowing, money, and power?
They only hold me captive and alone
Without love.

No need to talk about it, even to myself—
One touch of your hand reminds me that until now I
    was
Without love.

So let us wake up, joyful as this spring, birds singing in
    the sun,
Holding each other close, as if the world depended on
    our love,
For, in that state, we know that everything that is could
    never be
Without love!

CHAPTER 10

Awakening to the Scale and Urgency of the Challenge

We can stay with business as usual and watch our economy decline and our civilization unravel, or we can adopt Plan B and be the generation that mobilizes to save civilization. Our generation will make the decision, but it will affect life on earth for all generations to come.

LESTER BROWN, Earth Policy Institute

With or without love, with or without inner work for a change of consciousness, we must all confront the sobering reality of our generation. The future of humanity depends on how effectively and rapidly we mobilize all aspects of our life for one overriding aim—to save civilization.

One of the best governmental studies of just what this mobilization means is the Stern Review, commissioned by the British government and written in 2006 by Sir Nicholas Stern, the former chief economist of the World Bank. He concluded that the best scientific advice was that the levels of greenhouse gasses must be stabilized at less than double their pre-industrial levels. He estimated that this could be accomplished—if we all start seriously and without delay—at a cost of one percent of global domestic product, or GDP, a year, or half of what is currently spent globally on the military (nearly half of which is spent by the USA). The cost of inaction, he warned, will be at least five times higher.

Let me give one example, with acknowledgements to KarmaTube, of an American company whose CEO awakened to the challenge of becoming not just legally but actually green. "As Ray Anderson was preparing to give a speech at Interface, the billion dollar carpet company he founded, he had a stark realization. 'I was running a company that was plundering the earth,' he recalls. While Interface fully complied with the law, Ray knew that wasn't enough. So he challenged his employees to find ways to turn it all around, and forestalled objections from his own stockholders. 'He bet his entire company,' remembers one colleague. And the bet paid off. Today, Interface has cut fossil fuels by 45%, reduced water usage by 49% and slowed its landfill contribution by 80%. Plans are underway for it to be a fully 'restorative enterprise' by 2020. Oh, and along the way Interface has saved over $336 million."

No one has framed the practical issues for North Americans more cogently or produced a better plan of action than Lester Brown and his team of researchers at the Earth Policy Institute in Washington, D.C. As former President Bill Clinton has written, we must all heed Lester Brown's advice. At the same time, I cannot see how changes in human behavior of the magnitude Brown thinks are necessary can possibly be accomplished if there is not a major evolutionary shift in human consciousness to sustain these changes. On this aspect of the challenge, Brown has nothing to say. I believe that the outer actions and the inner developmental awakening must go hand in hand and support each other. There must be mutual respect for those whose talents are more directed to the outer tasks and for those who are primarily "working on themselves." As the scale of the challenge becomes more apparent, more and more people are going to be called to work on both the outer and the inner at the same time. Only on this basis is a broad global coalition viable.

I strongly recommend that you read Lester Brown's latest book: *Plan B 3.0: Mobilizing to Save Civilization*. You can download it free at http://www.earth-policy.org/Books/PB3/pb3book.pdf.

At the very least, read the flyer prepared by the Earth Policy Institute, reprinted below. I am including this flyer in the text of my book, rather than in the Appendix, because I think it is so important for you to read it. If you think the picture is overdrawn, study the voluminous notes in the book and consider the hard but reasonable options he is proposing, at an estimated annual cost of only one-sixth of the world's military expenditures in 2006.

PLAN B 3.0: MOBILIZING TO SAVE CIVILIZATION

http://www.precaution.org/lib/08/prn_plan-b.3.0.080116.htm
From: Earth Policy Institute, Jan. 16, 2008
By Lester R. Brown

"In late summer 2007, reports of ice melting were coming at a frenetic pace. Experts were 'stunned' when an area of Arctic sea ice almost twice the size of Britain disappeared in a single week," writes Lester R. Brown in his new book, *Plan B 3.0: Mobilizing to Save Civilization* http://www.powells.com/biblio/1-9780393330878-0 (W.W. Norton & Company).

"Nearby, the Greenland ice sheet was melting so fast that huge chunks of ice weighing several billion tons were breaking off and sliding into the sea, triggering minor earthquakes," notes Brown, President and Founder of the Earth Policy Institute, a Washington, D.C.-based independent environmental research organization. These recent developments are alarming scientists. If we cannot stop this melting of the Greenland ice sheet, sea level will eventually rise 23 feet, inundating many of the world's coastal cities and the rice-growing river deltas of Asia. It will force several hundred million people from their homes, generating an unimaginable flood of rising-sea refugees.

"We need not go beyond ice melting to see that civilization is in trouble. Business-as-usual is no longer a viable option. It is time for Plan B," Brown says in Plan B 3.0.

"Plan B 3.0 is a comprehensive plan for reversing the trends that are fast undermining our future. Its four overriding goals are to stabilize climate, stabilize population, eradicate poverty, and restore the earth's damaged ecosystems," says Brown. "Failure to reach any one of these goals will likely mean failure to reach the others as well."

Continuing rapid population growth is weakening governments in scores of countries. The annual addition of 70 million people to world population is concentrated in countries where water tables are falling and wells are going dry, forests are shrinking, soils are eroding, and grasslands are turning into desert. As this backlog of unresolved problems grows, stresses mount and weaker governments begin to break down.

The defining characteristic of a failing state is the inability of a government to provide security for its people. Somalia, Sudan, the Democratic Republic of the Congo, Haiti, and Pakistan are among the better known examples. Each year the number of failing states increases. "Failing states," notes Brown, "are an early sign of a failing civilization."

"Even as the accumulating backlog of unresolved problems is leading to a breakdown of governments in weaker states, new stresses are emerging. Among these are rising oil prices as the world approaches peak oil, rising food prices as an ever larger share of the U.S. grain harvest is converted into fuel for cars, and the spreading fallout from climate change."

"At the heart of the climate-stabilizing initiative cited above is a detailed plan to cut carbon dioxide emissions 80 percent by 2020 in order to hold the future temperature rise to a minimum. This initiative has three major components—raising energy efficiency, developing renewable sources of energy, and expanding the earth's tree cover. Reaching these goals," says Brown, "will mean the world can phase out all coal-fired power plants."

In setting the carbon reduction goals for Plan B, we did not ask "What do politicians think is politically feasible?" but rather "What do we think is needed to prevent irreversible climate change?" This is not Plan A: business-as-usual. This is Plan B: an all-out response at wartime speed proportionate to the magnitude of the threats facing civilization.

"We are in a race between tipping points in natural and political systems," says Brown. "Which will come first? Can we mobilize the political will to phase out coal-fired power plants before the melting of the Greenland ice sheet becomes irreversible? Can we halt deforestation in the Amazon basin before it so weakens the forest that it becomes vulnerable to fire and is destroyed? Can we cut carbon emissions fast enough to save the Himalayan glaciers that feed the major rivers of Asia?"

Although efforts have been made in recent decades to raise the efficiency of energy use, the potential is still largely untapped. For example, one easy and profitable way to cut carbon emissions worldwide is simply to replace incandescent bulbs with compact fluorescent bulbs that use only a fourth as much electricity. Turning to more efficient lighting can reduce world electricity use by 12 percent—enough to close 705 of the world's 2,370 coal-fired power plants.

In the United States, buildings—commercial and residential—account for close to 40 percent of carbon emissions. Retrofitting an existing building typically can cut energy use by 20-50 percent. The next step, shifting to carbon-free electricity to heat, cool, and light the building completes the transformation to a zero-carbon emissions building.

We can also reduce carbon emissions by moving down the food chain. The energy used to provide the typical American diet and that used for personal transportation are roughly equal. A plant-based diet requires about one fourth as much energy as a diet rich in red meat. The reduction in carbon emissions in shifting from a red meat-rich diet to a plant-based diet is about the same as that in shifting from a Chevrolet Suburban SUV to a Toyota Prius hybrid car.

In the Plan B energy economy, wind is the centerpiece. It is abundant, low cost, and widely distributed; it scales easily and can be developed quickly. The goal is to develop at wartime speed 3 million megawatts of wind-generating capacity by 2020, enough to meet 40 percent of the world's electricity needs. This would require 1.5 million wind turbines of 2 megawatts each. These turbines could be produced on assembly lines by reopening closed automobile plants, much as bombers were assembled in auto plants during World War II.

In the development of renewable energy resources, Brown notes, we are seeing the emergence of some big-time thinking—thinking that recognizes the urgency of moving away from fossil fuels. Nowhere is this more evident than in Texas, where the state government is coordinating an effort to build 23,000 megawatts of wind-generating capacity (the equivalent of 23 coal-fired power plants). This will supply enough electricity to satisfy the residential needs of over 11 million Texans—half the state's population. Oil wells go dry and coal seams run out, but the earth's wind resources cannot be depleted.

Solar technologies also provide exciting opportunities for getting us off the carbon treadmill. Sales of solar-electric panels are doubling every two years. Rooftop solar water heaters are spreading fast in Europe and China. In China, some 40 million homes now get their hot water from rooftop solar heaters. The plan is to nearly triple this to 110 million homes by 2020, supplying hot water to 380 million Chinese.

Large-scale solar thermal power plants are under construction or planned in California, Florida, Spain, and Algeria. Algeria, a leading world oil exporter, is planning to develop 6,000 megawatts of solar-thermal electric-generating capacity, which it will feed into the European grid via an undersea cable. The electricity generated from this single project is enough to supply the residential needs of a country the size of Switzerland.

Investment in geothermal energy for both heating and power generation is also growing fast, notes Brown. Iceland now heats nearly 90 percent of its homes with geothermal energy, virtually eliminating the use of coal for home heating. The Philippines gets 25 percent of its electricity from geothermal power plants. The United States has 61 geothermal projects underway in the geothermally rich western states.

The combination of gas-electric hybrid cars and advanced-design wind turbines has set the stage for the evolution of an entirely new automotive fuel economy. If the battery storage of the typical hybrid car is doubled and a plug-in capacity is added so that batteries can be recharged at night, then we could do our short-distance driving—commuting to work, grocery shopping, and so on—almost entirely with cheap, wind-generated electricity. This would permit us to run our cars largely on renewable electricity— and at the gasoline-equivalent cost of less than $1 per gallon. Several major automakers are coming to market with plug-in hybrids or electric cars.

With business as usual (Plan A), the environmental trends that are undermining our future will continue.

More and more states will fail until civilization itself begins to unravel. "Time is our scarcest resource. We are crossing natural thresholds that we cannot see and violating deadlines that we do not recognize," says Brown. "These deadlines are set by nature. Nature is the timekeeper, but we cannot see the clock."

The key to restructuring the world energy economy is to get the market to tell the environmental truth by incorporating into prices the indirect costs of burning fossil fuels, such as climate disruption and air pollution. To do this, we propose adopting a carbon tax that will reflect these indirect costs and offsetting it by lowering income taxes. We propose a worldwide carbon tax to be phased in at $20 per ton each year between 2008 and 2020, stabilizing at $240 per ton. This initiative, which would be offset at every step with a reduction in income taxes, would simultaneously discourage fossil fuel use and encourage investment in renewable sources of energy.

"Saving civilization is not a spectator sport," says Brown. "We have reached a point in the deteriorating relationship between us and the earth's natural systems where we all have to become political activists. Every day counts. We all have a stake in civilization's survival."

"We can all make lifestyle changes, but unless we restructure the economy and do it quickly we will almost certainly fail. We need to persuade our elected representatives and national leaders to support the environmental tax restructuring and other changes outlined in Plan B. Beyond this, each of us can pick an issue that is important to us at the local level, such as phasing out coal-fired power plants, shifting to more efficient light bulbs, or developing a comprehensive local recycling program, and get to work on it."

"It is decision time," says Brown. "Like earlier civilizations that got into environmental trouble, we have to make a choice. We can stay with business as usual and watch our economy decline and our civilization unravel, or we can adopt Plan B and be the generation that mobilizes to save civilization. Our generation will make the decision, but it will affect life on earth for all generations to come."

CHAPTER 11

It Will Not Be Easy, But It Is Not Hopeless

Unless a grain of wheat falls into the ground and dies, it abides alone: but if it dies, it brings forth much fruit.

JOHN 12–24

Yes, I wish to be and to act in ways that help to save our planet and our civilization. And yet, I realize that too often my wish is more a hopeful intention than a promise. I cannot, in good conscience, promise so much more than I can do or be.

But I can try not to be a hypocrite. I can walk to the store, instead of driving there. I can take a reusable shopping bag with me, so as to avoid using plastic bags that last forever in the dump. I can recycle my garbage. I can change my remaining light bulbs—you know the litany. Even my failures to remember can strengthen my underlying intention to awaken—when I suddenly remember and have a moment of remorse. And as our collective intentions gather momentum, we help each other to remember more often. I begin to change when I no longer accept the immutability of my old self. I see that it is old and worn out. With the help of your intention added to my own, I am almost ready to shed my grub self and take off as a butterfly. I feel its new aliveness in me already. It's not just about me. It's humanity as a species that is changing, no matter how many times I, like you, forget. Our genuine collective intentions inform that enormous shift. We are no longer alone but in good company.

As the Climate Crisis Coalition put it on November 20, 2007:

> It is hard not to feel despair these days. The U.N. IPCC has issued its grimmest report to date. It states unequivocally that climate change is upon us, the consequences will be serious no matter what, and to avoid calamities of an almost unimaginable scale, the world community must take draconian measures to reduce greenhouse gasses: all increases in emissions must stop within seven years, to be followed by a rigid course of sharp reductions—reductions that hardly seem possible given the ever-growing consumption patterns of the world....

> But there is hope. Just as we in the U.S. have witnessed this year a revolution in public concern, awareness, and determination to act, the world around us is waking up to the climate crisis.

Similarly, that redoubtable spiritual warrior, Joanna Macy, has written in *Taking Heart in Tough Times:*

> The most remarkable feature of this historical moment is not that we are on the way to destroying our world—we've actually been on that way for quite a

while. It is that we are starting to wake up, as from a millennia-long sleep, to a whole new relationship to our world, ourselves, and each other. This is the great and necessary adventure of our time.

If you have not seen the YouTube video, "The Most Terrifying Video You'll Ever See" http://www.youtube.com/watch?v=zOR v8wwiadQ, I recommend that you take a look. It makes the case for trying to do something about climate change more cogently and simply than anything I have seen before. It lays out the options on a small grid that proves conclusively that trying to do something about it is better than not trying, whether climate change by human actions is for real or is not. We have so much more to lose by failing to try than by trying. So why don't we?

Today, the most common excuse for not trying is that it is already too late. It's a lost cause. We are already done for, finished. You can take that on the authority of the Gaia man, James Lovelock and the astonishing Stephen Hawking. Start looking for another planet to colonize with our DNA, if we can, Hawking advises. Gaia is a goner. How about Mars? Call NASA. They seem interested in that option.

The shock effect of these views can, I suppose, be useful in waking people up to the seriousness of our situation, but fortunately there is nothing approaching a scientific consensus behind these counsels of despair. So let us not be in any hurry to abandon Gaia. Good planets—even a bit damaged—are hard to find. The truth is that we simply don't know what is going to happen. We need to remember that, as the world-renowned theatre director Peter Brook has pointed out, "Not knowing is not resignation. It is an opening to amazement." There is near unanimity among scientists that we need to make the best of the planet we have, instead of looking for others where a very few of us might take refuge and start breeding. I vote for staying here and doing what we must to save this lovely planet. It's our home and always will be for most of us, even if a few couples manage to fly elsewhere. Let us join the indomitable Helen Keller in saying, "I rejoice to live in such a splendidly disturbing time."

When we start looking for new technologies to replace or supplement the old ways of making gas for our cars, it is tempting to jump on the heavily promoted biofuel bandwagon. It is indeed possible to turn corn (and other grains) into fuel, but please remember that there are serious disadvantages that the American farm lobby does not tell you about. The production of most biofuels from corn produces five times more carbon emissions than ordinary gas-fueled production, and it drives up the price of food dangerously around the world. On July 4, 2008, *The Guardian* published a leaked World Bank study estimating that biofuels have pushed food prices up about 75% - not just 3% as in an official American study. I don't want my tax dollars to subsidize starvation in poor countries, as they are in the USA. Ethanol from sugar cane in Brazil makes more sense, but in the USA and Canada we must look elsewhere for solutions.

For those who have been close to despair, unable to see how we can still avoid the catastrophic effects of global warming, there are now some reasons for hope that these effects can be mitigated to a much greater extent than we would have thought possible at an earlier stage. Mitigation strategies are mostly modeled on making artificial clouds to reflect back into space some of the incoming heat from the sun. The United States Air Force has been experimenting with reflective particulates, including sulphates scattered from planes over wide areas in what they call Project White Shield. The Project is still classified so we don't know exactly what they are doing, but I have seen their broad white trails across the sky in New Mexico. At least locally, they are reported to have had a measureable effect in lowering the temperature in New Mexico and over much of the Caribbean. However, the concern of scientists (especially in Europe) is that sulphates released in the troposphere are further eroding the already depleted ozone layer and that this is allowing more ultraviolet to reach the earth. Much of the blight killing pine forests in Colorado and beyond may be due to the extraordinarily high UV levels now recorded, rather than to the pine beetles. The sooner we are told what the American Air Force is spraying the better. The destruction of more of the ozone layer would be too high a price to pay for all life on this planet.

Another experiment, a civilian project called Global Cooling, proposes to spray a fine mist of seawater into low clouds from a fleet of small unmanned wind-powered satellite-controlled vessels. Initial modeling suggests that this might be feasible within as little as five years, and that the global cooling required to counteract the warming from the current CO_2 levels might be achieved for as little as $100 million per year. The project is made up of a group of collaborating scientists headed by Dr. John Latham [at the National Center for Atmospheric Research (NCAR) in Boulder, Colorado] who first published the idea in *Science* magazine in 1990. Global Cooling is a project of Planetwork, a California not-for-profit directed by James Fournier.

Both these schemes—and any others that may show up—could, if pursued on a global scale, buy us more time to drastically reduce our carbon emissions over the coming decades and postpone the tipping-point after which it really will be too late to save our civilization. We obviously need that time. Our risk is now so high that almost anything that looks hopeful and affordable should be tested in real life. Any further delay is gambling with our survival.

Collectively, we have come a long way from where we were only three or four years ago. We now acknowledge that global warming is not only real—and caused mainly by human behavior—but that it is imminent and potentially catastrophic. But a lot of us, especially among the old-timers, are still not at all sure that the catastrophe can be averted, even if, starting now, we all did everything that we should to change what we are doing to the earth. Many analysts feel that forces much too big for us to handle have been set in motion while we slept and these forces of nature are becoming unstoppable more quickly than we are waking up.

It's time we listened less to doubting elders and more to the next generation, the generation of my grandchildren. They are the ones who are going to have to live with the consequences of the mistakes of omission and commission made by my generation, and they are beginning to play their naturally creative role as they face the problems we have made for them. They are not,

I find, wasting their energies on blaming their elders but are pushing all of us to act before it is too late. The first major student-based Power Shift/Energy Action Coalition Conferences took place at the University of Maryland and on Capitol Hill in Washington, D.C., in November, 2007, with the participation of 9,000 students. One of the students, Ted Glick, summarized the conference in an email:

> We don't just want policy fixes, or simply a change in leadership in the White House, higher fuel economy standards, or 80% emissions reduction by the year 2050. This movement is about more than just politics. This movement is about more than just supporting clean energy sources. This movement is about recognizing the patterns of consumption, patterns of thought, patterns of behavior that have led to the social ills we see today. It's about rediscovering the value of our resources, the value of our neighbors, the value of life on this planet.
>
> Our hope for the future absolutely is green: a connection to the green, life-giving force of our Mother Earth. A green, clean energy economy that gets us off the dirty fossil fuels which are destroying the ecosystem and are the reason for the U.S.'s wars of occupation in the Middle East and elsewhere trying to control oil and natural gas. A green, clean energy revolution that creates millions of jobs, lifts people out of poverty, strengthens communities and reduces the power of destructive corporations.

Along with these students, I believe that all of us want new values and new solutions. We can all be grateful to people like Lester Brown (see the previous chapter) and George Monbiot, *The Guardian's* brilliant columnist, for making the case so comprehensively and convincingly that global warming can either be stopped, or, at worst, contained within limits that would still give the inhabitants of Planet Earth a fairly comfortable and secure future.

In the 2007 Canadian edition of his best seller *HEAT: How to Stop the Planet from Burning,* Monbiot shows us exactly how it can be done, analyzing in convincing detail the specific steps we need to take in each of the main categories of our carbon-emitting activities to transform our homes, our public and private transport systems, and the policies of corporations and governments. I am also grateful to him—and to Lester Brown—for coordinating a vast amount of research which I therefore need not duplicate here. Step by step, category by category, they have shown us our future and proved it to be both possible and tolerable—if (and here is the rub) we follow their recommendations without procrastination, and follow them not only in Britain and the United States but also (and here is another rub) throughout the entire world. Our human tendency to put off for tomorrow what we know we should do today will still be there. But it should now be much harder for governments (and individuals) to put off action on the grounds that still another Commission or another study is needed because we don't know exactly what to do.

What Monbiot clearly implies, but does not say explicitly, is that the cumulative effect of doing all the things he recommends is that this would change us—the "lifting of global consciousness to a higher level" that Al Gore spoke of when he heard he had won the Nobel Peace Prize in 2007. Monbiot has the honesty of one who is awake and dedicated to the awakening of the rest of us. He does not pull his punches or gloss over the difficulties. He knows that intellectual analysis, which he does so well, is not going to be enough. This is how he concludes his brief:

> For the campaign against climate change is an odd one. Unlike almost all the public protests which have preceded it, it is a campaign not for abundance, but for austerity. It is a campaign not for more freedom but for less. Strangest of all, it is a campaign not just against other people, but also against ourselves.

My only complaint with both Monbiot and Brown is that they do not more explicitly insist that, in addition to all these things we must do, we must also work on ourselves to change ourselves, which means changing our consciousness. Perhaps, like Al Gore in the past, they do not want to talk too much about "raising consciousness." Why raise the bar that is so dauntingly high already?

I do so because I know from my own failures how difficult it is to change my habits, which are part and parcel of the prevailing culture in which I am embedded and asleep. Awakening progressively to this fact, I begin to awaken others, and their awakenings help me towards more freedom from the prevailing cultural hypnosis.

I can do so only because I am convinced by personal experience that we live in a reality larger than the visible material

one, that we "live and move and have our being" in consciousness—as fish live in water .We live in the air and consciousness
is in the air, as it is in our food and water and everything that
has life. Aware of it or not, we are part of the evolution of consciousness on this planet and we are therefore part of a cosmic
field of intelligence that seems, from a human perspective, to
need humanity to become more conscious. The better we understand this need and tune ourselves to its service, the more
help, in the form of energy, we will be able to receive from
the air we breathe and from the food we eat and the water we
drink.

CHAPTER 12

The Scientist Who Was Right—Unfortunately

It was, I suppose, normal for people to disbelieve the dire predictions of the few brave scientists who were trying to warn us twenty-five years ago of the ecological crisis they saw coming. What is not normal is that one of the most prescient of these early scientific whistle-blowers has narrowly survived several assassination attempts, and is still marginalized even today, without the grudging recognition usually given to those whom time has proved to have been remarkably correct in their forecasting.

This former protégé of the late R. Buckminster Fuller opted, at Fuller's suggestion, to pursue the practice of science as a comprehensivist and "not to let this global vision with which you are gifted die an overspecialized death." His name is Adam Douglass Trombly and he has indeed maintained his "global vision," Indeed, since that conversation with Fuller in 1969, Adam has expanded his focus from astrophysics/cosmology to include those fields of scientific study that are relevant to understanding the earth and all that humankind has done to her.

Moreover, Adam is not just a scientist. He is also a Tulku, an emanation of the great Tibetan promulgator of the ecumenical tradition, Jamyang Khyentse Wangpo. Adam was recognized by another emanation of that same mind stream, H.H. Dilgo Khyentse Rinpoche, when the two men first met. It is his perhaps unique combination of scientific and spiritual insights that has allowed Adam to come to a perspective that is very relevant to this book. Here we see, in one man's example, the fruit of an awakening that combines rigorous science with rigorous spirituality, practical action in the world along with the contemplation of wholeness. No one has a better track record of predicting, early and accurately, the dire consequences of global warming and telling us what we should do to mitigate them. His cosmological ideas are at the cutting edge of the new paradigm that is emerging—the paradigm that, I believe, will finally reconcile scientific and traditional cosmologies in a new life-sustaining world view for the 21st century.

By the time I met Adam in 1987 he had already accomplished a number of noteworthy achievements.

The first was the co-founding of Project Earth in 1979 with his friend and mentor, R. Buckminster Fuller, with the goal of comprehending, and then communicating to others, the actual state of the earth's environment without the dogmatic and political filters that so often corrupt the clarity of science. One of their founding principles for Project Earth was that they should never draw attention to a problem without, at the same time, having a solution to offer.

The first of these "solutions" was Adam's co-invention of the Closed Path Homopolar Machine, International Patent Number WO/1982/002126, with Joseph Kahn. This was another significant milestone—a major breakthrough on the road to escaping from the ecological consequences of our unsustainable fossil fuel economy, since it produced several times more electrical power than it consumed. But the United States government quickly stopped its development with a gag order in 1983. Two weeks later Adam's mentor, Buckminster Fuller, died.

The next year, Adam was named an R.J. Reynolds Scholar. It was this endowment that allowed his work to continue and provided for the survival of Project Earth against all the odds.

Then, in 1985, an Indian atomic scientist, Paramahamsa Tewari, who was then the Head of Quality Control at the Tarapore Atomic Power station in Trombay, India, used the description of the art disclosed in the 1982 Patent Document for the Trombly/Kahn Homopolar Generator to build a facsimile in India. Even though this machine was not as advanced as Adam's had by then become, Tewari reported an output/input ratio of 260% in the March, 1986 issue of the American journal *Magnets*. It was the first time that claims of power output greater than 100% had ever been physically verified by a bona fide third party working from the description of the art in a patent document.

As a result of the gag order on his generator, Adam spent most of 1986 working as the Director of the Greystone Institute in Evergreen, Colorado, with a Bulgarian ex-pat scientist, Yul Brown. Brown had rediscovered the extraordinary characteristics of the stoichiometric mixture of hydrogen and oxygen gas as derived from water through electrolysis, based on the work of German scientist Vicktor Schauberger in the 1940's.

After seeing Adam's demonstration of the perfect combustion/implosive-detonation of hydro-oxy gas three times, the Chairman of the Board of a major oil company was quoted as saying, "This will be the end of oil." As we all know, it was not. Instead, Adam lost his job at Greystone and the hydro-oxy project was sabotaged out of existence.

In spite of these difficulties, by 1987 Adam was in great demand on the international lecture circuit, for he was able to explain and forecast trends in the global atmosphere and geosphere better than anyone else. His controversial approach to global climate modeling had attracted both the praise of some and the ire of many conventional scientists. He did not simply speak about the "greenhouse" effect. Adam was the first to use the term "global climate destabilization" along with several other terms that are now in general use. In lectures and radio and television interviews throughout the world, he revealed the reality and the causes of global ozone depletion beyond the narrow focus on the Antarctic "ozone hole." In 1987, the year that I met Adam, he traveled one hundred and sixty thousand miles disseminating the messages of Project Earth.

So the Adam Douglass Trombly I met in New York was already familiar with the intrigues and sorrows of this troubled planet. He was articulate, incisive, and at times too outspoken for his own good. During an early conversation with Adam, I suggested that he should learn to be more diplomatic. Since then, he has taught me to be less diplomatic.

Not long after our first meeting Adam introduced me to a remarkable phenomenon in physics, which he claimed was quite possibly the source of the disproportionate output/input ratios of some of the technologies he invented or co-invented. This field of energy, he told me, pervades everything, everywhere. In physics, it is called the Zero Point Vacuum Fluctuation Background Field. In 1962 the legendary physicist, the late John Archibald Wheeler, wrote in the annual *Review of Modern Physics* that the mass equivalent energy potential of this field is 10^{93} grams per cm^3. However, the thought that the energy of this field is accessible in any practical way is antithetical to the way reality is still understood by most physicists.

Even in his teens, Adam had seen a direct link between the zero point field and all manifest existence. Rather than being an empty void, space is, as he puts it, "pervaded by unfathomable energy, which is <u>not</u> the artifact of a 'big bang' but the field in which the implosion that preceded something like a 'big bang' or 'grand inflation' was originally potentiated."

In Adam's cosmology,

> Infinity, which is infinitely present everywhere ... ultimately overwhelms or outshines any and all gravitationally bound masses or (for that matter) subjective psychophysical phenomena.
>
> In the midst of Infinity, all worlds and all modifications of the all pervading field relax back into our true source and substance. This universe is increasingly no longer gravitationally bound. The expansion of this universe will continue to accelerate until the illusion of separation from the Infinite will simply not be supported on any level whatsoever. Levity overwhelms gravity. Scientists on this planet are just beginning to glimpse the reality of this Field and realize that this Presence is inescapable.
>
> The Infinite cannot be left out of the equation. The Infinite is the ultimately equilibrating Force. The Infinite is not properly describable by a shadow cast

in time and space referred to by some scientific humorists as the "dark energy." The Field of our appearance here is not subject to abstraction or being intrinsically broken into singularities. Being is seamless. Phenomena come and go ... arise and dissolve. Ultimately, we come to realize that the "dark energy" is anything but dark.

Most of my colleagues find it disconcerting when I refer to the "Boundless Luminosity of Infinite Space" as acting upon or directly impacting all temporal/phenomenal modifications of this Presence Field in a manner that is ultimately liberating and is at the root of existence itself. However, the data do not lie. This universe is transforming/dissolving in an accelerating momentum in the midst of Infinity and this undeniable fact stands as a stark testimony to the non-intrinsic nature of separation. You see, there is nothing the scientific ego or any other assertion of singularity can do about it!

These challenging enigmatic statements about the nature of reality are more likely to resonate with spiritual practitioners than with conventional scientists who conveniently dismiss the credibility of a man who has no scientific degrees. But Adam has to his credit too many practical scientific accomplishments to be easily dismissed. I have already mentioned his zero point energy generator. Take earthquake prediction, as a less esoteric example.

In September/October of 1987, Adam, with colleagues Elizabeth Rauscher and Bill Van Bise, accurately forecast the Whittier earthquake in Los Angeles, California, using extremely low frequency signal analyzers to observe pre-seismic disturbances in the earth's resonant magnet field. More than a week prior to the quake, Adam had been interviewed by ABC radio news in that same city and had predicted that a major earthquake would soon hit the city. Officials at UCLA, where he was scheduled to do a major public lecture, were so upset by his prediction that they cancelled his talks. However, after the quake actually happened, Adam was invited back and proceeded to teach packed auditoriums about this new seismic forecasting technology and the broader ecological issues addressed by Project Earth.

I have personally observed the fact that Adam and his colleagues have accurately forecast several major earthquakes using this approach, notably the Loma Prieta/San Francisco Quake of 1989, the Scotts Mill/Portland Oregon quake of 1993 and the Northridge quake of 1994.

The Scotts Mill quake happened during Adam's work with the first Clinton Administration on Vice President Gore's National Performance Review. Adam interacted on a daily basis with the then Head of Strategic Planning for the United States Coast Guard, Captain Michael Egan. Egan was so impressed with the accuracy of Adam's forecasts that he took the matter to the press. However, even though Adam and his colleagues received very positive international press coverage regarding this and other successful forecasts, his method is still not used for the benefit of the public to this day. I am still asking: "Why not?"

In June of 1989, I found myself in New York again with Adam and his colleague David Farnsworth. After Adam's gag order had been dropped, he and David had further developed yet another type of novel zero point energy technology called the Piezo Ringing Resonance Generator. They had brought a small version of this remarkable device to New York where we demonstrated it at the United Nations.

After the demonstration and his speech that followed in Dag Hammarskjöld Auditorium at the United Nations, Adam received a sustained standing ovation from an international audience. During his speech Adam asked a senior engineer from the Boeing Corporation to either confirm or deny the 54-1 output/input ratio of the device. The Boeing engineer responded: "The device that was just demonstrated today actually works as claimed. There are no tricks and I do know what tricks to look for. I have spent several hours alone with this technology and all I can say is that it works. There is in fact nearly 54 times more electrical output than input. I don't know how it works but I have no doubt that it works."

That evening I felt uplifted, as I am sure did many others, with a new infusion of hope. We imagined that the world might change for the better from that day forward. It wasn't just the energy technology itself but the energy that so obviously pervaded us all on that day that opened our eyes, our minds and our hearts to the very real possibility of a much kinder and better world in the future.

The next Monday, Adam, David and I once again demonstrated the same device in the United States Senate Banking and Finance Committee hearing room in Washington. Once again it functioned superbly. However, only Senator Carl Levin and a handful of staff people actually attended. At the last minute, President George H. W. Bush, or someone close to him, had apparently ordered members of his National Security Council to call the nearly two hundred Senators, Congressional Representatives and members of their staffs who had already accepted our invitation and that of our sponsor, Senator Timothy Wirth. Suddenly they were invited to the White House for an "off the cuff discussion of the new Clean Air Act" with the President during the exact same time slot which we had scheduled for our demonstration the next morning. Naturally, they went to hear the President. We were denied the headlines we needed and had anticipated. Indeed, I must say sadly, we were intentionally pre-empted by the President of the United States!

What a pity! Our clean technology could provide clean air for the whole earth and all her people. It consumes no fuel. It requires no radioactive source material. It does not rely on the variable power of the sun or the wind. And it produces no greenhouse gases!

I have seen this technology work with my own eyes and I have also heard first hand the testimony of highly qualified, independent engineers who have lauded its performance! For the last twenty years I have been asking: "Why is this technology not powering the entire world today?" Instead of embracing this chance for an abundant and clean future, the world continued its descent into chaos. The next step was the Gulf War of 1991.

Immediately after that Gulf War, executives from Friends of the Earth International in Washington, D.C., who knew that I had once been the Canadian Ambassador to Iran and Kuwait, contacted me. They asked me to head a scientific mission to assess and document the environmental damage done to Saudi Arabia, Kuwait and the Gulf as a direct consequence of that war. Sir Paul McCartney had generously funded the mission.

I contacted Adam and he agreed to participate in the international team of scientists from France, Turkey, and the United States that was assembling. When several members of my team still had no visas for Saudi Arabia on the day before our departure, Adam was able to make a last minute request to his friend, the Saudi Ambassador in Washington, Prince Bandar bin Sultan. He graciously obliged, and we were off.

While in the Gulf, Adam played a major role, investigating and filming the incredible damage done by Saddam Hussein's incendiary demolition of more than 700 Kuwaiti oil wells. He also studied and filmed the unbelievable 11 million barrel oil spill in the Persian Gulf while our entire team flew on a large Saudi civil air patrol helicopter which we no doubt owed to Prince Bandar and the endorsement he had given us, along with our visas.

Adam's videotapes of the fires and the oil spill became a matter of some controversy with one official of the Meteorological Environmental Protection Agency of the Kingdom of Saudi Arabia. On the night before Adam's scheduled departure from the Kingdom, this Saudi official threatened him with immediate beheading "for espionage" if he did not turn over "the master copy of the tape." Adam walked down the hall of the building, accompanied by that official, to the Bechtel Corporation offices, which were housed there. There he asked a senior

Bechtel employee (to whom he had turned over his "master copy" earlier that day) to please hand the tape over to the official. After also being threatened with decapitation, the Bechtel employee did so. Then the official took Adam back to his personal office and threw the tape into the trash. When Adam protested that this was his scientific data, the official replied: "I will send you away with whatever I feel is appropriate."

Adam had had an intuition that things might get rough and had arranged for early passage that night out of the Kingdom. He flew back to London and then on to the Netherlands to meet me and provide both his testimony and an edit of his videotapes for an international press conference that Friends of the Earth International hosted in Amsterdam. Thankfully he not only got himself out of a serious predicament but also managed to get his original videotapes out of Saudi Arabia, having given the Saudi official a copy, not the master tape.

When I was preparing for our press conference in Amsterdam, little did I realize that Adam had stayed up very late the night before with some wonderful employees of the National Radio and Television Studios of the Netherlands who helped him re-edit the video footage and make copies for the international press corps the next day. The evidence exposed by our tape dramatically contradicted the official position of the Bush Administration in Washington that nothing serious was happening as a result of the oil fires and helped to persuade many other countries of the importance of getting them out as quickly as possible.

I have since learned that by the time Adam and I were flying back to the Unites States a few days later, nearly two billion people had seen some portion of our tape. Our message had found its way into Europe, Scandinavia, Russia, China, India, Japan and Australia. The proverbial cat was out of the bag.

When Adam and I arrived at Dulles International Airport, two officials from the US State Department approached us. When they requested that Adam turn over his tapes, Adam responded simply by saying, "Fine; you can have them but the contents of these tapes have already been seen by people all over the world. Only the United States and Canada have yet to view some portion of them." The senior official uttered an expletive, and walked away.

You may by now be wondering why both American and Saudi officials would be so upset by Adam's tape that they would do everything they could to prevent it from being shown. The answer to this and so many other Middle Eastern mysteries lies in one word: oil. Adam had filmed the black plume from the oil fires rising to nearly 20,000 feet, while on the ground U.S. and Saudi officials were insisting that it was not going above 2,000 feet and was therefore not likely to do more than local damage around Kuwait. But any scientist could see that if the plume was rising to 20,000 feet, the environmental consequences to the entire world could not be tolerated for the five years which the Americans were saying it would take their four teams of firefighters to get all the oil fires under control. In addition, the major oil companies of the world, the "Seven Sisters," were heavily invested in Saudi Arabia and not averse to seeing the Kuwait oil fires burn off the substantial commercial advantage they had over the Saudis due to the extraordinary gas pressures that made Kuwait oil so much cheaper to extract.

We released the tape to the United States press corps at our press conference at the National Press Club in Washington, D.C., the next day. As a result, portions of the tape were transmitted by every major broadcast and cable network, as well as by many specialty and local stations. Subsequently, National Geographic included some of Adams' footage in their IMAX film about the oil fires of Kuwait.

That same videotape (with Adam's narration) became a centerpiece for our testimony before the U.S. Congress. As a result of our testimony, and the plan for remediation that we presented to Senators and Congressional Representatives from both sides of the aisle, there was a six-fold increase in the number of teams who worked valiantly to put out the fires, which were actually extinguished in six months—not the five years that the original four American firefighting teams had testified that it would take them. Thus, untold damage to the atmosphere and the people of this planet was avoided.

Nevertheless, there was much suffering. In Bangladesh 143,000 people died in a monster typhoon that was catastrophically exacerbated by the dense effluent from the oil fires of Kuwait. The loss of those poor souls would have only been the tip of the iceberg, in terms of the disaster which could have befallen our planet if the oil fires had been left to burn for five years. We must also remember with gratitude the incredible bravery of more than 18,000 men from many different countries who successfully battled those fires. Those men truly deserve to be called heroes.

Our mission had in fact catalyzed the largest cooperative international environmental remedial action in history, though it was insignificant compared to the scale of international cooperation that is now required to mitigate the effects of global warming.

Next, I turn to another subject in which Adam has had a major role in my education. I have gradually become convinced that there are probably life forms other than us through whom Consciousness is making its presence known. To put it another way, God may have helpers from other planets in actualizing the plan. It seems to me altogether possible that there are more intelligent, more spiritually and technologically advanced cultures than our own, on other planets that we know not of, probably closer in actual realization to the Great Intelligence that pervades our Universe. In this perspective, we can take comfort in the fact that humanity is not facing this daunting crisis alone.

If what I said seems to you so outrageous that you are ready to stop reading, please don't. Let me make my case. It is a case based on my personal experience with an "unidentified flying object" (or UFO) that I have kept to myself until now for obvious reasons.

CHAPTER 13

Are There Really Off-Planet Cultures?

There are more things in heaven and earth, Horatio,
than are dreamt of in your philosophy.

SHAKESPEARE, *Hamlet*

"I have no problem with UFOs. I have seen one," said President Jimmy Carter in a moment of candor. I have too. Let me tell you about it. It has changed how I see the world and how I understand consciousness, in ways which—if they were shared by humanity more generally—would, I believe, help us to weather this stormy century.

On the Labor Day week end of 2002, I was at my log cabin on McGregor Lake, in Quebec, 25 miles east of Ottawa, with Tina Petrova, actress and filmmaker. We were, and still are, good friends—no more than that—brought together by a common love of the great Sufi poet and mystic, Rumi. I mention her name to show that I had an independent and sober witness to this experience. She can confirm that these almost unbelievable things happened, as I will now describe.

After dinner in the cabin, we went out to sit on the steps leading down to the lake to enjoy the gathering darkness as the first stars appeared. "Is that the North Star?" asked Tina, pointing to a bright star almost overhead. "No," I replied, "The North Star is over there. This one looks too bright to be a star."

Then the big "star" began to move. "Ah, a satellite," I commented. But immediately it turned sharply away, so how could it be a satellite in a fixed orbit?

We looked at each other. I was puzzled. But for Tina this was not her first encounter with a UFO and she suggested something I would not have thought of. "Let's see if it responds to our wishes. If both of us send it a strong inner signal to turn left…." The words were scarcely out of her mouth when "it" obediently altered course to the left, not in an arc but in a sharp right-angle turn. No more words were needed. We both held up our hands, high above our heads. Again instantly the "star" flew up, higher and higher above us. We brought our hands down to our laps and it turned on a dime and came straight down towards us, until we could see its saucer shape and lighted windows. We raised our hands to the right and it complied again. And even when it came quite close to us, it moved without making a sound, completely silently. It could even hover motionless in space, waiting for our next thought signal.

For the next forty minutes, by the clock, it played with us, showing us time and again that it could follow our thoughts, for how could our gestures be visible more than half a mile away in the darkness? It showed us that it could remain stationary in one place or move in any direction that we indicated. It was like a video game, where apparently Tina and I could control the movements of the circular craft that seemed to be about the length and breadth of a small plane, maybe forty feet across and sometimes only a quarter of a mile away from us. However, we were well aware that the control was not in our hands but in the telepathic minds of whatever beings were flying this craft from a world other than ours, with a technology that we had yet to master. By the time that it finally turned away without a signal from us and disappeared to the northwest, we were in a heightened state of attention. I would say that I was more awake, more alive, than at almost any other moment of my life. Too bad it could not last.

The next evening was also beautifully clear, and, as you might expect, we were on the dock again as night fell on the lake. Sure enough, along came our new friend or friends, once again ready to play with us, moving their craft exactly as we indicated for nearly half an hour. But this time they showed us a new trick: the whole craft could disappear whenever it wished to do so and reappear out of nowhere. It could choose whether to be visible or invisible to us. It appeared and disappeared several times and finally flew straight upwards until it vanished in the zenith from our sight. No air force in our world has this kind of stealth technology.

I was left wondering many wonders. Who were "they?" Could they be from some secret Royal Canadian Air Force research station experimenting with exotic new technologies? If so, why would they make themselves known to us, so close to Ottawa? Wouldn't they be avoiding curious eyes, rather than courting our attention? And, whatever their origin, why would they waste their time playing with us and showing us how superior their flight technologies and psychic abilities were, compared to ours? What were we supposed to do with this startling information? Who were they and where had they come from? What kind of acknowledgement did they want from us? What were they trying to tell us? Today, I am still wondering, but I am beginning to have some guesses.

Perhaps they simply want us to acknowledge their existence, and get us used to the idea of other civilizations existing on other planets, so they show themselves to people whose level of denial is less strong, who are more open to welcoming a relationship and not simply protecting their reputation by keeping silent—as I have for five years—so as to keep in the good graces of most of my friends.

But now, at my age, isn't it time to tell the truth, regardless? So I am belatedly following Rumi's good advice, given 800 years ago but still challenging: "Forget safety! Destroy your reputation! Be notorious!"

Both before and since that September weekend, I have met many people who have had similar experiences, and we have compared our wonderings in search of answers. Among others, I have been privileged to know Dr. Steven Greer, who abandoned his medical career to found and lead the Disclosure Project. In his documentation of a government cover-up lasting sixty years, I found photocopies of Top Secret memos signed by high level people in government, people whom I have known, including Dr. Omand Solandt, the head of the Canadian Defense Research Board in the 1950s, who clearly thought UFOs were real, and that the Pentagon wanted to keep their reality a secret. You can examine the evidence online at www.DisclosureProject.org. It is a website well worth visiting.

In particular, I draw your attention to the National Press Club presentations of the Disclosure Project in Washington, D.C., on May 9, 2001, and on November 12, 2007.

At the second presentation, in 2007, Fife Symington (former Governor of Arizona) and 14 pilots, senior military officers and high level government officials from seven countries testified, telling of their personal experiences of UFOs. I find their testimony both credible and impressive. You can find it at http://www.freedomofinfo.org/national_press.htm.

The first presentation, in 2001, drew a larger audience, I am told, than any previous National Press Club meeting. On this occasion, public testimony was given by former members of the United States military establishment, who had personally experienced both UFOs and the official cover-up. I found the testimony of Dr. Carol Rosin both credible and chilling. She had been the first woman CEO of an American aviation company in the 1970s and was a close friend of the famous NASA scientist, Dr. Wernher von Braun, who designed the rockets that took the Apollo astronauts to the moon.

In 1977, near the end of his life, von Braun privately charged Rosin to devote the rest of her life to stopping the spread of weapons into space, which von Braun saw as the greatest danger on the horizon. "For years," he told her, "the military-industrial complex that Eisenhower warned us about has been grossly exaggerating the military might of the USSR so as to get the Pentagon's budget inflated. When the Soviet Union collapses, outspent by America, then they will invent the threat of global terrorism. And, when that excuse becomes too transparent to be credible, they will claim to be defending us from extra-terrestrials, invading us in their UFOs—anything to keep the military-industrial complex in the war business that makes their money and gives them power."

Thirty years later, Carol Rosin is still dedicated to keeping space free of all weapons and to developing friendly relations with whatever off-planet cultures may be out there, concerned about our welfare and giving us every sign of being willing to help us through the perilous passage we are taking through this century. In March, 2008, the Prime Minister of Japan publicly declared that if a UFO showed up over their territory, Japan (unlike the USA) would not assume it had any hostile intentions.

Another voice that has been crying bravely in the political wilderness is that of the former Deputy Prime Minister and Defence Minister of Canada, Paul Hellyer. At the Exopolitics Symposium in Toronto on September 25, 2005, he stated "UFOs are as real as the airplanes flying overhead. That is my unequivocal conclusion." In an interview with the *Ottawa Citizen* on February 28, 2007, he pointed out that UFOs must travel vast distances to reach the earth and might have something to teach us about the advanced energy propulsion systems and fuels they are using. "We need to persuade governments to come clean on what they know. Some of us suspect they know quite a lot and it might be enough to save our planet if applied quickly enough," he said.

After Peter Jennings' special ABC TV program on UFOs had aired in 2005, he told Larry King that he had come to the personal conclusion that they were indeed real and had visited our planet.

In the first half of 2007, several stunning events have taken place with far too little public notice. The governments of France, Argentina, Mexico, Italy, Brazil, and the United Kingdom have released thousands of previously secret official sighting reports on UFOs that appeared over their territories during the past half century. These reports parallel and confirm the testimony of the military witnesses who testified for the Disclosure Project at the National Press Club in 2001 and 2007. There has been quite a stir on the Internet, but the mainstream media have slept through it as if nothing had happened.

Throughout the 20th century, anyone who thought earth was being visited by intelligent beings from other planets was automatically shunned as weird. But public opinion on this issue has been changing. According to the Roper Poll of 2002, 56 % of Americans believe UFOs are real and 67% think there are other forms of intelligent life in the universe. The percentages are higher among younger people and are probably still higher today, certainly in Europe, than they were in 2002. Denial isn't working. The governments of even some of our closest friends, like the United Kingdom and France, have given up the pretence. Why continue to devote so much official effort to maintaining a fiction, trying to explain away thousands of sightings reported from all over the world? Are we not grown up enough to cope with the news that we are not, after all, alone in the universe? Now that hundreds of other planets have been found in other solar systems—and it is generally assumed by astrophysicists that there are billions of them in the universe—any other view is beginning to look unreasonable.

Both the denial of the existence of UFOs and the denial of global warming should be jettisoned without delay by all the governments that have not done so already. That would assist the general awakening we need in order to survive. Without such action, governments will only alienate further the doubting populations they claim to serve and will therefore be in a weaker position to act effectively to modify the effects of climate change that are already being widely felt, such as hurricanes, earthquakes, floods, and heat waves never before experienced. We have just begun, I am afraid, to see the shape of worse things to come. It is high time to change course. If, as I too believe, "the government within the government" (as U.S. Senator Daniel Inouye of Hawaii has dared to call it) knows about some energy technologies of alien origin that could rapidly replace fossil fuels and save us from the worst effects of climate change, it is surely criminal for them to endanger the whole planet in the interests of maintaining American military domination. What is the use of dominating a dying planet when declassifying these technologies could save it, and all of us?

As I write in July, 2008, I commend to you the magisterial documentary that has just become available on the History Channel by the great Canadian director, David Cherniak. It is called *UFOs: the Secret History*, and it contains more inside information than I have found anywhere else.

The question about our UFO visitors that remains unanswered is: "Are we capable of acknowledging their existence and accepting their help?" If you can believe what I have told you of my own interactions with them at Lake McGregor, not to mention the testimony of high ranking military officers, such as Lt. Colonel Philip Corso, you can see that their energy and flight technologies must far surpass ours. In *The Day After Roswell*, Corso has described the beneficial technologies (including integrated circuit chips, fiberoptics, lasers and super-tenacity fibers) that he claims the American military has discovered by reverse engineering a UFO that crashed in Roswell, N.M., in 1947. In our search for innovative technologies to mitigate the effects of global warming, those "off-planet cultures" which made the huge silent UFOs that have been showing up all over the world might very well have helpful suggestions to make to us if we could bring ourselves to ask. There is no evidence I know of to suggest that our UFO visitors have any other interest in us than that of keeping a concerned eye on a younger civilization going through a hard period in its juvenile evolution. As for us, we need all the help we can get.

If all that I have written is insufficient to persuade you that there is something real about UFOs, because you have not had the direct personal experience of them such as I have reported, the next best thing to a close encounter is to see Suzanne Taylor's magnificent full-length documentary film, *Walking in Circles,* on the thousands of beautiful and complex crop circles that have appeared mysteriously in 40 countries worldwide, with the greatest preponderance found near ancient sacred sites in southern England. She shows differences between the crop circles made by humans trying to debunk the phenomenon, and the real thing which imprints sophisticated geometric forms on a crop field in seconds and as many as 35 of them in a relatively small geographic area in a single night. This film shows that there have been crop circles in England not just in the last thirty years but reported in the media of the day in the 19th century and earlier. Among the many commentators in the film who are familiar enough with the phenomenon to be fascinated by it, the late Pulitzer Prize-winning Psychology Professor John Mack of Harvard University is especially interesting in the way he calls us to open our minds to an intelligence beyond our human intelligence. You can also read his books, the best selling *Abduction* and *Passport to the Cosmos,* which tell about his work with people who reported abduction experiences. He initially studied these experiences in order to discover their pathology and was amazed when he could find none.

"If we were open to the intelligence that created these crop circles," Suzanne Taylor, the producer/director of the film, says, "we would not be plundering the planet and destroying one another. We would be one people engaged with what is larger than we are. It would be the biggest shift in our perception of reality since Copernicus and Galileo, and, as someone in the film says, it could be what saves us." To overcome our natural skepticism and official disinformation, we need to become aware of the mystery of the crop circles and prepare our minds to open to new dimensions of reality without further delay and obfuscation.

I have been privileged, as a diplomat at the United Nations, NATO, in the Middle East and South Asia, to have seen world events unfold from the inside. I have seen how often people are manipulated by lies from the most authoritative sources. Until a few years ago, I believed the lies that UFOs were figments of the imagination of demented people. I have heard the lies about countries and cultures "we" did not like. Let us never be deceived in the future by "leaders" playing on our paranoia, pointing to the heavens as the source of the next wave of "terrorists" from whom they say they wish to protect us. Only full disclosure will permit a rational policy to emerge from the confines of military secrecy where it is being maintained in the narrow national interests of military hegemony, and in the economic interests of inflated military spending. The cover-up is certainly not in the interests of the planet nor of the people whom the military are supposed to be protecting.

At the same time, let us not make the mistake of thinking that some benevolent Extra Terrestrials are going to save us from our human follies and solve all the problems that we ourselves are creating for ourselves and our planet. The ETs are surely not about to deprive us of the right to make mistakes—even fatal mistakes—as a natural part of our learning to be fully human. We must learn to be responsible, and to adapt to changing circumstances. We must also be awake enough and humble enough to recognize our need for help and to ask for help in the right way. Only those who learn these lessons are objectively worth helping.

CHAPTER 14

A New Paradigm for a New Century

I believe in God, only I spell it Nature.

FRANK LLOYD WRIGHT

The truly crucial limits confronting mankind are not outer but inner. It is not the finitude of the planet, but the bounds of human will and understanding that obstruct our evolution towards a better future.... We human beings are the cause of the problem, and only by redesigning our thinking and acting ... can we solve them.

ERVIN LASZLO

Despite the astonishing and accelerating growth of scientific knowledge, we still seem to be far from understanding the big picture. A "theory of everything" eludes us. We are between stories, and that is as uncomfortable as trying to sit down between two stools. As Thomas Berry has written:

The old story, the account of how the world came to be and how we fit into it is no longer effective.... Our challenge is to create ... a new sense of what it means to be human.

Could our difficulty be that we are still embedded in a world view that is too restrictive, too partial, and too materialistic? Are we still largely shackled to a view that reduces life to mechanics? This is a view of the world that diminishes consciousness to no more than the product of the brain, as the co-discoverer of the double-helix structure of DNA and Nobel Laureate, Sir Francis Crick, implied when he said bluntly, "The brain produces consciousness as the kidneys produce urine." If awakening means opening our eyes to a deeper and more inclusive understanding, we need to be brave enough to think the unthinkable and feel the unfathomable, even at the risk of turning the world that we think we know upside down. That is just what a paradigm shift does, time and again. Copernicus and Galileo could tell you about it. And now we can see that we are living through another shift that may turn our thinking upside down.

The world we think we know has been built on separation, starting at the bottom and putting separate bits together to make a sort of whole. Could we upend that way of thinking, starting not from the bottom but from the top, for a change— starting from the whole and working down to the parts? In this way, we would be taking a metaphysical instead of a physical approach. Popular wisdom says that the whole is greater than the sum of its parts. If this is true, and I believe it is, how can we expect to construct a whole from the bottom up, part by separate part? Is reality no more than what we can measure? And how about a quality that cannot be measured by our instruments or analyzed by our minds but can be known in our hearts, the way I know that I am?

The quantum world, our world, is not based on separation but on an interconnected unity of relationships in a plenum or a field of energy/information within which matter and energy are hopelessly entangled. That sounds more like wholeness to me—holons within holons, as Arthur Koestler once put it to me in London. So let me emulate him and try putting a new word on that wholeness: consciousness. I don't mean the consciousness that keeps me alive for a time, "my" consciousness. I mean the Consciousness with a capital C, the Consciousness from which my consciousness comes and to which it returns, and with which it may, from timeless moment to timeless moment, be in resonance when I am truly present. In India, my consciousness is called *atman* and the Consciousness is called *Brahman*; in their wholeness, they are one, not two. In other great cultures, other words are used, such as the *Tao* in China, or the Buddha Nature in Tibet—different words, but one wholeness, one field, with many levels within that field. All traditions agree: the field is omnipresent (if we speak in terms of space) and eternal or timeless (if we speak in terms of time). But the term omnipresent implies infinite space and eternal implies infinite time, and science still has difficulty with immeasureable infinities. We have not yet come to a common understanding between the sages, the metaphysicians, and the physicists.

The essential disagreement is about consciousness/Consciousness and the meaning of wholeness. For the majority of scientists, consciousness is secondary, a product of the human brain. For the sages of every persuasion, it is primary. Not only the brain but every form of life—all matter and all energy—comes from Consciousness and returns to Consciousness. That kind of unity or wholeness is very different from what the scientists are talking about when they speak of the interconnectedness of everything. Both can speak of the "seamless robe" of reality, but they understand those terms very differently.

It is my contention—and I know it is contentious—that scientists are embarrassed by three fundamentals of reality: *consciousness, infinity, and eternity*. In an objective world of matters and energies that they can measure, scientists are lost in the limitless immeasureability of these terms that they tend to dismiss as metaphysical. Only the bravest scientists are beginning to admit their embarrassment, at least in private conversation although rarely in print. Most are typically in denial, defending out-dated paradigms inherited from the assumptions of their predecessors, rather than exploring new dimensions of possibility that would stand reductionist materialism on its head, and that might offer a fresh way out of the awkward complications and paradoxes, for example, of multidimensional string theory and cosmological inflation theories. When, or if, a satisfying theory of everything is eventually discovered, my guess is that it will feature consciousness as an omnipresent field, which relates space to infinity, and time to eternity. It will look a lot more like the traditional metaphysical model than the present scientific "standard model."

I am hoping that the next generation of cosmologists in physics will pay more attention to exploring the traditional model for clues that could expand their view and assist them in awakening to a solid theory of all and everything, of inner as well as outer experience. For, in our present culture, we are less likely to pay attention to our priests than to our scientists. May our scientists exercise their authority more wisely than did the priests when they had authority. May our scientists not become the new priesthood, defending an obsolete paradigm! May they bravely pioneer the general awakening!

The paradigm shift cannot be confined to the domain of the sciences, the outer world. It must also revolutionize the inner world and the worlds of religion and spirituality. Here also pioneers are needed. In the religious and spiritual world, we can see two views in conflict. The old view clings tenaciously to the forms—dogmas and texts—of the past. The new view sees spirit or presence as primary, and asks that forms be adapted to the promptings of a higher Intelligence that sees what is needed for a new time and new conditions. After all, the old familiar forms came into common use in the past because they helped people to stay open to that Intelligence. It was often for lack of a continuing connection with that higher Intelligence that the forms were given or took the place of a real inner sense of authority. When a prophet or messenger died, his or her words were all that remained—unless their successors had learned how to hear authentic living guidance directly from above and by doing so, adapt the forms to new conditions as times changed, without distorting either the intent of the founder or the purity of the teaching. Historically, we can see that most often this was only possible through esoteric schools, usually sheltered in seclusion; and even there the pull towards a literal fundamentalism has always been strong.

Today the challenge is for the living sources of esoteric spirituality to begin to participate and cooperate more openly in the solution of the problems now threatening our very survival. More and more people are attracted to this new spirituality as the old economic and political structures begin to collapse. This new spirituality can draw people from all the old religious traditions and from among those scientists who have found the confines of contemporary science in academia or industry too restrictive in their search for truth.

With the additional pressures of global warming growing every year, the new spirituality can only increase, as more and more people find, even on the Internet, effective ways to wake up and to make use of the frictions of daily life to renew their awakening.

Changing our worldview matters because that is how the world can be changed. With the old view dominant, we can see where global warming is taking us in the present passive drift towards the ecological cliff. A new view—an awakening—is vital if humanity is to have a future. Listen to environmentalist Andrew Beath, author of *Consciousness in Action*:

> Our human worldview has always been evolving; it is evolving NOW. We are on the cusp of a new perspective, an awakening that is the next step in the evolution of Human Consciousness. A successful navigation of today's planet-wide dangers requires a bridging from our current perspective to a worldview that embodies a deepened understanding of the nature of reality. Participation in this process is a path that adds meaning and beauty to one's life.

What is needed now is a worldview broad enough and deep enough to encompass and attract the spiritual progressives and the scientific free spirits, along with those in the religious community who are ashamed of the narrowness of the fundamentalists, of all persuasions, who have persuaded themselves that there is no salvation outside their own divisive brand of dogma and belief.

In this chapter, I have used words such as Tao and Buddha Nature to represent the one field of wholeness and unity. In the next chapter, we explore a view of the one Field that might meet the requirements of progressives and free spirits of every persuasion, and thus facilitate the transition to a new world that is becoming not only possible, but necessary.

CHAPTER 15

The Akashic Field—A Big Step Toward Wholeness

Everyone who is seriously involved in the pursuit of science becomes convinced that a spirit is manifest in the laws of the Universe—a spirit vastly superior to that of man, and one in the face of which we, with our modest powers, must feel humble. In this way the pursuit of science leads to a religious feeling of a special sort.

ALBERT EINSTEIN, in a letter of January, 1936,
Albert Einstein: The Human Side

In the previous chapter, I have called the Field of Fields, the underlying reality of all that is, Consciousness. In the 19th century, most Western scientists would have preferred to call it "the luminiferous ether." Tibetan Buddhists might prefer "the boundless luminosity." Einstein said simply, "I want to know God's thoughts—the rest are details." Today, cosmologists call it the quantum vacuum or the Zero Point Field. An empty vacuum of nothing it is not. It is super-dense, yet super-fluid; and it contains far more energy than the entire physical world of matter. J.A. Wheeler's calculation is 10^{93} grams per cm^3. Some physicists have suggested that "plenum" would be a better term than vacuum. Moreover, they say that the energy that this plenum contains in such abundance is coherent and intelligent, full of information, endlessly self-organizing and creative, the origin of all manifested forms, and perhaps, as Ervin Laszlo has suggested, the holographic storehouse of the world's memory.

In *Science and the Akashic Field,* Laszlo has given the Unified Field of physics an ancient and honorable Sanskrit name. "Akashic" means "ether" or space, containing the other traditional elements (air, fire, water, and earth) with the connotation of radiating brilliance or light. For Newton, the universe was basically mechanistic; for Einstein it was relativistic; and for Laszlo it is morphogenetic. His Akashic Field provides an integral ground of everything. I am proposing that this Field can also be called Consciousness. In Buddhism it is called the Buddha Mind or Buddha Nature. As far as I am concerned, you can call it Life, or Love, or God, or Tao, or Brahman or any other word for greatness, provided only that you use this word as a synonym for the Great Unknown. For it is only with this humble attitude that we can open our own little particle of consciousness to some form of contact with the higher levels of Consciousness. Such an attitude is surely a precondition of our awakening to the imminent reality of that higher Presence.

For a Muslim, 99 names are not too many for the one God. Each age needs to find its own words for God; and all of them are only our little fingers pointing feebly towards the greatness of the unknown Absolute.

In addition to Ervin Laszlo, I have great respect for the late David Bohm's attempts to point us towards an underlying holographic reality of order that he calls "implicate," as distinct from the observed outer or "explicate" order of reality. Today the deeply "entangled" nature of the quantum world can be understood as an example of what Bohm calls the unfolding and enfolding of the implicate order, interacting with the explicate order that we can see.

Following the pioneering work of Francisco Varela and Lyn Margulis, some of the leading current researchers in biology are bringing us the same story, although using different metaphors. Mae-Wan Ho likens the amazing capacity of cells and organs to work together in a living organism to the way members of a good jazz band spontaneously improvise together. Our understanding of the world has changed a lot since I was at Esalen in the late 1970s, listening to Gregory Bateson talk about an "ecology of mind." Now Laszlo can tell us that consciousness is "not fully possessed by the individual, but is present throughout society and perhaps humanity as a whole....The next evolution of our consciousness ... is in the direction of transpersonal consciousness, a consciousness of unity with others and oneness with nature."

I agree with the direction of Laszlo's thought but I would say that what I earlier called Consciousness is even more fundamental than what is currently called "transpersonal consciousness." *Consciousness, energy, and matter* could become our new Trinity. What Meister Eckhart called "the ground of Being," I would call Consciousness with a capital C—the top of the ontological line. This, for me, is what Laszlo is now calling the Akashic Field, which is (in his words) "a cosmic information field (that) connects organisms and minds in the biosphere, and particles, stars and galaxies throughout the cosmos."

To understand the mystery of consciousness, we may need to turn to the poetic insights of the great Persian-speaking Sufi mystic, Jellal al-din Rumi. One day he was on a boat with some fishermen when they spotted a large school of fish gathered, as if in conference, below them. "What are they conferring about?" asked Rumi. "Are they considering the possibility that they are surrounded by something they don't see but which we, from where we are, call 'water'?"

Are we, like those fish, unaware that we are living in Consciousness? As fish live in water, we live and move and even write books in the all-pervasive field of Consciousness, and are as mystified by it as the fish in the story must be by water. Like them, we are too much in it to be aware of it.

To become aware of the omnipresence of Consciousness may be the next great leap in human evolution and the foundation of the new paradigm in which both science and spirituality can find common ground. For consciousness is the field that connects—not separates—everything with everything, at all levels, and everything with the All, in one Wholeness.

Can we now begin to see our emerging wholeness? To see in how many different ways we sing the same song, dance the same dance, the dance of life? In all the suffering that is an inevitable part of the greatest crisis humanity has ever faced, it is when we feel, not only our suffering but, at the same time, the thrill of our tentative awakenings, as if they were the turning of a page in the story of human evolution. This is the story of the evolution of consciousness.

To conclude this chapter, let me quote from a recent newsletter of the Institute of Noetic Sciences, which for three decades has played such a seminal role in bringing awakening into the mainstream:

> Over the past several decades, new scientific discoveries along with a surge in grassroots initiatives addressing social and economic injustices have begun calling into question the view of the universe—and essentially of ourselves—as ultimately cold and mechanistic. Revealing both the mysterious directionality of the evolving cosmos and the irrepressible humanity within our own natures, new evidence is emerging that we are innately capable of far more than we realize. Yes, the evidence is compelling that the arc of the human species is on a self-destructive decline, and yet once the pieces are put together, there is no denying that another reality is fighting through the cracks of the dominant narrative. We are just beginning to tap into our potential as human beings despite, or perhaps because of, the multiple crises that we are facing.

CHAPTER 16

Where Does Help Come From?

My help cometh from the Lord who hath made heaven and earth.

PSALM 121

We lie in the lap of immense intelligence, which makes us receivers of its truth and organs of its activities.

R.W. EMERSON, *Self-Reliance*

Our ancestors knew where their help came from. We seem to have forgotten, at just the time we most need to remember it. When only the Higher can save us, it's time to reopen, if we still can, our portholes on the Infinite, closed by our own egoistic illusions of divinity. Those who most vociferously deny the existence of God are often, it seems to me, unconsciously trying to usurp the place of God for their own inflated selves. But we are not standing on the highest branches of the tree of being. When we awaken to our lowly station, we will improve our chances of receiving the help we so badly need.

Now that so many of us in our culture have been alienated from any kind of God, perhaps it's time, as I suggested in the previous chapter, to use a less theological term for the Highest—and call it Consciousness. But you may feel that it is a stretch to equate the quantum vacuum, the plenum, with that Consciousness. Of course, I am not saying that it is conscious the way *we* are conscious. That would be no less reductionist and anthropomorphic than the ancient image of God as a man with a long white beard. It is Consciousness. I am speaking of eternal infinite space, always and everywhere omnipresent in the universe we can see or imagine, and far beyond. According to our foremost scientific scouts, that reality is vastly energetic, supremely intelligent, full of information and creatively morphogenetic. The chances are millions to one that life itself comes from that vacuum and returns to it, for life is a form of energy and energy cannot be lost. Where else can it come from and go back to? Traditional wisdom unanimously endorses that conclusion.

I have already quoted Rumi's insight in the last chapter. Except at special moments in our lives, we are not aware of this consciousness because we are in it, as fish are in water. Ervin Laszlo's son Christopher has something similar to say in his father's book, *Science and the Akashic Field*. "It is as if all the fish and plants in the fish tank were physical manifestations of the water, interconnected by the water in such a way that whatever happens to one influences all the others, in a mutually dependent system evolving together in a delicate dance of all life and all of nature."

It would be naïve and self-centered in the extreme to believe that humans are the only conscious life forms to emerge from this source. We now know that there must be many billions of planets in the billions of solar systems in the billions of galaxies. Don't you think that it is extremely likely that many of these billions of planets could have conditions favorable to life, as on our planet? Don't you feel that there are most probably many other forms of intelligent, self-aware life elsewhere in the cosmos? If that is the most likely scenario, why would we assume that human life on this planet, on the periphery of our galaxy, had uniquely developed the highest forms of technology in the universe?

Does it not follow that there may be many gradations of reason embodied in life forms, some of which might be capable of visiting our earth and keeping an eye on our slowly evolving ability to match our technological progress with an equivalent inner growth in conscience? Given the myriad of life forms that we can scarcely count on our own planet, might there not be more evolved beings than we are elsewhere in the cosmos, who could be "God's agents," so to speak, capable of helping us in our hour of need, provided we awaken enough to suspect their existence and ask for their help? We're probably not the first planet on which dominant life forms have caused serious trouble in their juvenile years.

As Einstein famously reasoned, we cannot expect to correct our problems with the consciousness that created them. In other words, real change can only come from a consciousness higher than the one that runs our ordinary life. In us, that higher seems to reside in what we call the subconscious. And how that consciousness communicates with our ordinary waking consciousness is a great mystery. There are times when we all, knowingly or unknowingly, may have experienced some form of higher intuition from what I am calling Consciousness. If you have had glimpses of that kind of help and would like to be more open to it, look first for guidance from one of the pioneers of higher consciousness among our own species. Some of those pioneers have been priests or spiritual teachers; some have been scientists, like Einstein. They can help us to become more sensitive and more open to a higher part of our mind, a deeper understanding. As we search for this and become more free of the obstacles on the path, we should always aim at tuning ourselves to a sensitivity that would permit us to be aware directly of what comes from a particle of consciousness in ourselves, not through any intermediary teacher. If "God helps those who help themselves," we must each, to the best of our own abilities, vigilantly work to wake up. Surely that must be a precondition of our receiving any help from "above."

At the risk of over-simplifying very complex and mysterious interrelationships, let me offer this personal distillation of traditional Wisdom. This as a way of looking at the relativity of being and consciousness, and the need for both, in our evolving world of form, starting from the Highest and coming down the great Chain of Being.

1. THE UNMANIFEST, or the Unknown Ground of Being.

2. CONSCIOUSNESS, or the omnipresent quantum vacuum or plenum.

3. Awakened consciousness. As embodied in the great Prophets and Teachers.

4. Self-consciousness. The awareness that is in us in moments of presence.

5. Our "waking consciousness." What ordinary sleeping people like us call it.

6. Animal consciousness. Remember that we share 99% of our DNA with some animals, so we have an animal consciousness, too.

7. Plant consciousness. Have you ever hugged a great tree and felt its life?

The evolutionary shift of consciousness now required by Nature and currently in process is, as I see it, moving level 5 people, as they begin to awaken, into level 4, at first in moments of what we call presence and then potentially on an enduring basis. Similarly, I would suppose, those at level 4 also have a chance to break through at times to level 3 and from there to what, a century ago, was called cosmic consciousness on level 2.

In *A New Earth,* made famous by Oprah Winfrey, Eckhart Tolle sees this shift of consciousness as imperative for our survival. "The dysfunction of the egoic human mind, recognized already more than 2,500 years ago by the ancient wisdom teachers and now magnified through science and technology, is for the first time threatening the survival of the planet. Until very recently the transformation of human consciousness … was no more than a possibility, realized by a few rare individuals here and there, irrespective of cultural or religious background. A widespread flowering of human consciousness did not happen because it was not imperative." Now it is.

As both Eckhart Tolle and Gurdjieff have pointed out, there seems to be a cosmic need for more awake people, so that some fine energy that the earth desperately needs at this time can pass through them. For that need to be met, human consciousness must now evolve rapidly. That is our good fortune, if we are trying to wake up now. There is good anecdotal evidence that more people are indeed awakening now, perhaps more than in any previous time, but we do not yet know whether enough will wake up soon enough to meet the cosmic requirement. If they don't, Gurdjieff's successor, Madame Jeanne de Salzmann predicted emphatically, "the earth will fall down." However, if the planetary requirement is met, instead of a collapse, there will (as the Book of Revelation promises) be "a new heaven and a new earth." Breakthrough, not breakdown. And it depends on us, for those now alive are the decisive generation!

In the 20th century, human evolution was largely focused outward and we began to awaken to the prospect of becoming a space-faring species in the 21st century, reaching out not only to the moon but to Mars and beyond. At the same time, as André Malraux and Einstein (among others) foresaw, we need to balance these outward awakenings with an inner awakening in this 21st century, a spiritual awakening of both conscience and consciousness. Instead of keeping our collective attention fixated on our exciting outer discoveries, we now need to attend also to the inner being that each of us is in essence, so that we can become more sensitive to the finer—more conscious—energies which science is just beginning to explore. For it is our inner relationship with these energies, including this omnipresent but almost entirely unknown Consciousness, that will determine whether or not

humans can adapt their behavior to the cosmological imperatives of Great Nature—and therefore whether or not humans
will survive on this planet.

Emerson (and the American Transcendentalists of the 19th
century) understood this, calling that omnipresent consciousness "an immense intelligence," which we serve, whether or not
we are aware of it, as "organs of its activities." In our own time,
Paul Hawken has sounded the same note in *Blessed Unrest*:
"What will guide us is a living intelligence that creates miracles
every second, carried forth by a movement with no name."

It is the power and the intention of that intelligence—the
power of presence NOW—that animates the global movement
with no name, and makes our impossible task possible. We
will astonish the old pragmatists and realists who "knew" human beings could never change—being unaware that we are
all changing all the time. We will even surprise ourselves, as we
awaken to who we are and why we are here at this time.

Already in 1991 I had a lesson in what five environmental scientists and a retired diplomat could accomplish when we were
serving what was needed by the planet. As I have mentioned
in Chapter 12, this little team of the International Friends of
the Earth managed to expose the extent of the danger if the
international community had allowed the Kuwait oil fires to
burn. Had they burned for the five years that the four original
American teams were planning to take to get them out, the
atmosphere of the planet would have been seriously polluted.
Against all the odds and in spite of death threats, we aroused an
international effort by more than twenty-four teams who put
out the fires in six months. It surprised us too. It taught us that

nothing is impossible if the call to action comes not from self interest but from the needs of the Whole.

Why have I taken the trouble to write this book? In my ninetieth year, I have no need to make a name or make money. I am writing only because I have been called to write, and indeed helped to do so, once I had overcome my laziness and resistance to the call. All those who, however reluctantly, have obeyed a real call are, in one way or another, helped. I am in no way an exception. That seems to be the rule, whether or not we can understand how it works. Test it yourself.

Where we can easily go off track, however, is in embellishing the help we have been given and adding too much of our own invention. To avoid that mistake, I must stop when the help stops. That is why this is a *little* green book. I offer it to you, unknown friend, with all the warmth of my being. It can help you to wake up to the extent that I have been helped, in writing it, to wake up too. We are in this together. We are all now co-responsible for creating, while we still can, a new heaven and a new earth, here, where we are. And the cosmic clock is ticking. Will we awaken before it is too late? Will our generation rise to the occasion or sleep through it? Our children and grandchildren will know the answer. We—all of us now alive—are the tipping point generations. For us, our most urgent obligation—and I would call it a sacred obligation—is, at the very least, not to make the task of those who follow us impossible.

As we begin to realize that all real help, all creativity, come to us from a higher source, I am indebted to Johannes Brahms and his biographer, Arthur Abell, in *Talks With Great Composers,* for this concluding quotation:

> To realize that we are one with the Creator, as Beethoven did, is a wonderful and awe-inspiring experience. Very few human beings ever come into that realization and that is why there are so few great composers or creative geniuses in any line of human endeavor. I always contemplate all this before commencing to compose. This is the first step. When I feel the urge I begin by appealing directly to my Maker and I first ask Him the three most important questions pertaining to our life here in this world—whence, wherefore, whither? I immediately feel vibrations that thrill my whole being. These are the spirit illuminating the soul-power within, and in this exalted state, I see clearly what is obscure in my ordinary moods; then I feel capable of drawing inspiration from above, as Beethoven did.... Straightaway the ideas flow in upon me, directly from God, and not only do I see distinct themes in my mind's eye, but they are clothed in the right forms, harmonies and orchestration. Measure by measure, the finished product is revealed to me when I am in those rare, inspired moods ... when the conscious mind is in temporary abeyance and the subconscious is in control, for it is through the subconscious mind, which is a part of Omnipotence, that the inspiration comes. I have to be careful, however,

not to lose consciousness, otherwise, the ideas fade away....

Then the ideas which I was consciously seeking flowed in upon me with such force and speed, that I could only grasp and hold a few of them; I never was able to jot them all down; they came in instantaneous flashes and quickly faded away again, unless I fixed them on paper. The themes that will endure in my compositions all come to me in this way. It has always been such a wonderful experience that I never before could induce myself to talk about it—even to you Joseph. I felt that I was, for the moment, in tune with the Infinite, and there is no thrill like it.

CHAPTER 17

A Theory of Everything, for Everyone

One must strive to understand: this alone can lead
to our Lord God.

G.I. GURDJIEFF, *Meetings With Remarkable Men*

A spirituality that is only private and self-absorbed,
one devoid of an authentic political and social consciousness, does little to halt the suicidal juggernaut
of history. On the other hand, an activism that is
not purified by profound spiritual and psychological
self-awareness and rooted in divine truth, wisdom,
and compassion will only perpetuate the problem it
is trying to solve, however righteous its intentions.
When, however, the deepest and most grounded
spiritual vision is married to a practical and pragmatic drive to transform all existing political, economic and social institutions, a holy force—the
power of wisdom and love in action—is born. This
force I define as Sacred Activism.

ANDREW HARVEY

Before I conclude, I want to try to put into words what I
have come to at this point in my life, and what I think we
are all collectively coming to, as a consensual idea about the

nature of ultimate reality, inner and outer—the emerging new worldview. I offer it to you, my fellow "seeker of truth," so that you may critique it, and I sincerely hope you will improve on it, for that is how humanity evolves. Only when we come to share a common story or paradigm can we think and feel and act together. We need a new theory of everything that both science and tradition—everybody in every culture—can accept as a 21st century worldview.

At the moment we seem to be stuck where Einstein and Bohr left us seventy years ago. After Bohr had discovered that two electrons having a common origin are able to exchange information about their states instantly, even when they are light years apart, Einstein pointed out the obvious absurdity of this contention. Then Bohr knocked this fast ball out of the park by replying, "But you are assuming that these electrons are separate."

In the same way, dear reader, you and I are still assuming that we are separate. You are somewhere else right now, as I write these words in an earlier time and a different place, and we naturally think we are quite separate from each other. But if, for a moment, we take stock of the possibility that the life or being that animates each of us may have come from the same great source of life and being (just as those electrons came from the same atom), then we must admit that we are not as separate as we had thought. This means that there is some sense in the contention of most physicists today that everything is connected and dynamically interacting in a Wholeness from which, as I see it, everything came and to which everything returns. We might, for now, agree to call that wholeness "life" or "being" or "consciousness;" but what is more important than our names for the Unknown is that it is, so far as we now know, One.

If this much is generally agreed, by both science and traditional teachings, then let me look as deeply as I can into my own experience of life or being or consciousness, looking beyond those labels towards my direct experience of what I actually am now. Looking merely at my brain, my feelings, and my bodily instinctive functions is not enough; I must look for that which is aware of all these functions, standing behind my feelings and thoughts, as an awareness that sees them. That awareness is carried by the body but is not the body, does not come from the materiality of the body, but from higher up the great chain of being, carrying a higher or finer vibration. And it is only that awareness that can say "I AM" with conviction, with truth. Indeed, the God of the Old Testament said as much when asked what He should be called: "I am that I am."

Such an evocative metaphysical principle only resonates in those who can relate it to their own personal experience. Looking at the outer world, science recognizes four basic forces: gravity, the electromagnetic force, and the strong and weak forces. When we look at our inner worlds, all of us, if we pay attention to the sensation of gravity, can feel it in our feet or our buttocks. Most of us can probably sense flashes of the electromagnetic force in our body electric. But I doubt that many of us could say that they have direct personal experiences of the strong or weak forces.

I like Gurdjieff's definition of understanding as "acquired from the totality of information intentionally learned and from all kinds of experiences personally experienced." Unless our ideas and our sensations can be correlated in a partnership of knowledge and being, they are simply borrowed from the experiences and speculations of others and are of little value in constructing a deep personal understanding of ourselves and of our world, a "worldview" that can inform our understanding consciously and guide our actions and relationships.

To be meaningful, metaphysical principles must be grounded in our personal experience. What resonates actively in me is my experience of what I am calling "awareness." When an active attention connects my consciousness with a higher consciousness, if only for a moment, my whole body resonates with this vibration. If it does not resonate in you yet, please keep looking for it, as if it was there—because it is. You can come to feel it, as I do, as our very beingness, yours and mine. It is the real you, which you have, subconsciously or sometimes consciously, been wishing to be for years. How do I know that? Because I have the same beingness energy in me as you do, as every being does in different degrees. It is as if we all shared the same ground of being, the same "I," but each conditioned functional "me" is different—the "I" coming from the stars, the "me" from this planet. This is our dual nature, one part of conscious divine origin and potentially immortal, the other functioning mechanically and destined to return to the dust from which it came.

This being that I am—that you are—is palpable only when I am present, now. That is why being here now is so important. "Now is the being of time," wrote Heidegger at his most obscure. "But as it is 'no more' or 'not yet,' there is no being."

If we were fully human beings, we would live now in our be-ingness, not only in our thoughts about what was ('no more') or what might be ('not yet'). If we were fully human, our ex-periences of the present moment (the eternal moment) would include past, present and future as a Unity. It is our habit of thought that separates these times in us, and it is our being that unites them.

But now I open my eyes and see the world around me. I see other embodiments of this awareness on the vast scale of being that lies before me, whether I turn my attention to other living beings around me, to the forests and mountains in the distance or to the vastness of the starry sky at night. Did all this come from the One and was it manifested by the One? Can we know or intuit to some extent what is the nature of that One? Or are we constrained to remain silent about that which is beyond our knowledge—and, I would add, above our level of being?

While there is no denying that the lower cannot see or un-derstand the higher, the great spiritual teachings, ancient and modern, are in agreement about at least two basic truths:

First, that there is something in each human being that has the potential of seeing at least one level above and one level below the level in which "we live and move and have our be-ing," as St. Paul puts it, and second, that this potentiality can be developed by certain practices that are found in the eso-teric schools within each of the great teachings and may well be much older than any of them.

In my long life and through my fortunate contacts with sev-eral traditions, most notably with the Gurdjieff teaching and with the Dzogchen practices of Tibetan Buddhism, I can say that I have, to some extent, verified these two truths and have seen them verified in the lives of other practitioners I have known in these ways. I know that some practices work and others do not. It is not a matter of having faith of any kind. This is my pragmatic conclusion based on my experience. But you will have to verify it for yourself, taking nothing on faith, from me or from anyone else.

From a practical point of view, it is more important to know that it works than to know why or how it works. Yet the mind will always raise objections until it knows why and how. Western medicine was scornful of Chinese acupuncture, for example, until Scotty Reston of the *New York Times* had to have his appendix surgically removed in Beijing using acupuncture for anesthesia. This demonstrated that acupuncture worked. Only later did Western medicine discover how it worked—that acupuncture releases endorphins in the brain that mask the pain.

So, if by experience, we discover that something in the air can be absorbed by a person who is attentively aware, which is not absorbed by someone who is just automatically associating, then to practice paying attention to my breathing, moment by moment, becomes of much greater practical importance than to understand the mechanisms by which this happens. However, since the mind keeps wanting to know how it works, let me share with you my personal guesses.

Since I have found in myself a sensitivity or an awareness that is gradually transforming my experience of myself and of the world, I would like to understand what constitutes this awareness, which has such beneficial consequences. Could this awareness be, indeed, what I am in essence—could it be myself, or even my Self? Is my being in fact a particle of the beingness from which all embodied beings come? And have I been embodied in order to serve the purposes of the Being of Beings, according to laws that give me the chance of evolving to a more conscious level of awareness?

By personal observation and experience, I have concluded that there is something in the air we breathe that, when I am fully attentive and present, is capable of enlivening all my functions and giving me a feeling of well-being, as well as a clarity of mind that I do not ordinarily experience. Then, what is it that is the active ingredient in what I describe as air? Is it one of the known components of air or is it something I can know only indirectly, by drawing inferences from the results in me of this mysterious but ubiquitous something? What is it, we might hypothesize, that is everywhere but is imperceptible to our senses, even when they are extended by all the latest technologies? To use an ancient word, this something is ineffable. Yet it is palpable. I feel it and I cannot doubt that my inner experience of this mysterious something is real.

When I look outward, as I am now, is my experience different? Or do I find the same mystery as I found when I went searching inwardly? Just as the air inside and outside an empty cup is the same air, reality outside my skin can hardly be different from my inner reality. What I find on my inner search is "I Am" and "awareness." These words, I feel, point to the same reality and that reality does not stop at my skin—it is everywhere. I also call it life, being, and consciousness. Are these different names for different aspects of the same omnipresent vibration or energy?

For example, take being—a rather amorphous word for most of us—certainly for most scientists. The terms "disembodied being" might fit better with what seems to be a ubiquitous Field that includes everything. As St. Augustine would say in theological terms, "There is nowhere God is not." Could we say that there is nowhere Being is not?—or Life? or Consciousness? Surely we can. It would at least be difficult, if not impossible, to sustain the opposite contention: that there is nowhere life is—though reductionist science sometimes comes close to it! Even if the experience of Life too often eludes me, I can surely sense in my body just now the life that I have consciously breathed in a moment ago. I feel a love for that life, and think clear thoughts that I never had before—thanks, it would seem, to this "something" in the air. Surely that must be what activates me so miraculously when I remain present and vigilant, silent and still, not allowing my attention to be hijacked by any passing thought or reaction.

Logically, I cannot prove that life, or being, is the omnipresent active element that can transform my consciousness, but I cannot disprove it either. Experimentally (if I am persistent) I can prove to myself that saying to myself "I Am" as I breathe in and out can have, for a time, the desired effect. It works. I become more present. So why must I prove it logically?

Everything that I have said about being, I could also say about life or about consciousness. Are they all, as the Buddhists would say, simply "fingers pointing to the moon," and are we in danger of confusing the fingers for the moon? For me, it helps to think of these three Western-style attributes of the Absolute—life, being, and consciousness—as related to the different parts or centers of the human organism, which all great teachings recognize as the microcosm of the Whole. On this scale, consciousness is related to the mind; being to the body; and life to the feelings. But each one of us is all three, in different proportions. Every Trinity reflects what in some traditions is called the Law of Three: the action of active, passive and reconciling forces.

Whatever horrors may be attributable to this or that religion, most religious and spiritual practices are designed to promote an inner awareness of self that is compassionate and unitary, not violent and separate. It is never *my* self versus *your* self. This inner awareness is the basis for the love of my neighbor and of all sentient beings. This is the foundation without which there can be neither harmony nor justice nor peace—either among peoples or within myself. We simply go on making the mistake of assuming that we are separate, because our bodies are. But the being that I am and that you are is not divided. We are One in being.

The existential error of our times is that I think that I *am* my body, just because I *have* a body. When I see and feel that I am *in* my body, I am much closer to awakening. No metaphor can speak adequately of a higher level of interconnection, but, if we accept the quantum view, I suspect that, in this higher dimension, we are essentially like cells in the organism of the One. In front of the Unknown, I am silent; but I am still aware that I am.

CHAPTER 18

Working Together to Save the Planet We Love

When I look inside and see that I am Nothing,
That is Wisdom.
When I look outside and see that I am Everything,
That is Love.
Between these two my whole life turns.

NISARGATTA

Had he lived today, Hamlet would affirm with more conviction than ever: the question is, to be or not to be. He would be right. But it is not the skull of an individual that Hamlet would ponder, but the living earth. Will we survive on this planet, or become extinct like the dinosaurs?

ERVIN LASZLO

This final chapter is about what we know, in contrast to the preceding chapter which was mostly about what we don't know. On the basis of what we know, it is time to take a decision and act.

We humans know that if we do not mend our ways, our planet—or at least a quarter of its life forms, including us—may die in the foreseeable future.

We know what should be done to mitigate, if not avoid, this disaster. We know that our civilization must stabilize emissions of greenhouse gases by 2015, begin to reduce them shortly thereafter, and bring them to zero by mid-century. Most of the mitigating technologies needed to do so are already available and affordable. For example, tapping into less than one percent of the available solar and wind power would power the whole world sustainably.

We know how our global institutions and our economic system could be transformed to serve planetary, rather than corporate requirements—the public, rather than the private, good.

We know that, if we act decisively now, we can still look forward to a reasonably comfortable life for our descendants and that the total cost is affordable—much less than we now spend senselessly on war and only a quarter of what we now spend on oil and gas. We also know that if there is much more delay in taking decisive action globally, the cost will go up precipitously and a secure outcome for humanity can then no longer be guaranteed.

We know that, in the atomic age, war has become obsolete and nuclear war insane.

We know that, even on a damaged planet, there is enough for everyone's needs but not enough for our greed.

We know, more than ever before, how to change ourselves, our behavior, our lifestyles, our consciousness. We have recently discovered (or rediscovered) that our minds and our bodies are far more adaptable than we had thought.

We know that we now have the means, through the Internet, to spread all that we know, about ourselves and about the world, globally with remarkable speed and at minimal cost.

Knowing all that we know,
why don't we act accordingly??

Nothing is stopping us—nothing except some ideas that have taken over our minds and dominate our belief systems about the world and about ourselves and what we think is possible, about what we can do or become. Yet we also know that human beings can change their core ideas and values, and that this can change humanity. It is time we did just that, first individually and then collectively!

Other civilizations have collapsed in different places in the past, but there has never been a global collapse, and there has never been a collapse in which the participants had complete foreknowledge of both the problem and the solution *before* the collapse became inevitable, yet did not do enough to avert it. Are we destined to be the first civilization in human history, knowing all that we know, to collapse through inertia, striding over the cliff in our sleep as if we were hypnotized lemmings, while knowing all the time that we could wake up and find everything needed at hand?

As we contemplate that very real possibility, confronting the irrationality of our inertia honestly and sincerely, is there not an instantaneous revulsion in our hearts, a determination to make a personal commitment that we will do everything in our power, now and for the rest of the life that is given us, to avoid such an unacceptable stupidity and to save the planet we love? That awakening has already begun. To facilitate it in ways appropriate to each of us is, from now on, our moral responsibility.

For some this will mean social and political activism; for others it will mean researching how to transform our ways of making energy so that our economy no longer depends at all on fossil fuels; for others it will mean a dedication to inner transformation so that a higher energy can reach our planet through more sensitive human vehicles. As the urgency of our actual situation awakens our collective consciousness, there may be many more ways still to be discovered that will inspire our creativity and focus our attention where it is most needed. Ideally, we should aim at combining contemplation and action, but this may not yet be humanly possible for us all. For the rest of us, we must do what we really can—no more excuses or delays.

Through the hard times ahead, we will have to learn that there is no one way of saving the planet. There are a multitude of ways. If we are to work harmoniously together—as we must—we need to recognize this diversity and respect each other's very different ways of contributing to the common goal.

When we realize where we are and what is needed to change course, will a critical mass of humanity wake up in time?

Yes! Yes! We must, we can, and we will.

YES WE CAN! YES WE CAN! YES WE CAN!

That is no longer an American political slogan. It has become a moral imperative for everyone, everywhere.

A Tibetan Exchange About Awakening Awareness

Now that I have completed this "Little Green Book on Awakening," I am wondering about your experience of the journey we have been on together. In particular, I am wondering whether you have been trying the inner exercises that I have suggested as aides to awakening, and, if you have, what you have found. Naturally, I would be overjoyed to hear that you felt you had been enlivened and enlightened by what I had proposed. But from long experience I know that for most people it takes a long time and a lot of trying before they discover——usually when they are not trying at all——anything approaching a breakthrough to another kind of mind, another level of awareness. In some traditions, this is called non-dual or non-conceptual awareness, in which there is no judgment and no associative commentary——just a direct immediate awareness of what is happening, uncluttered by any thoughts about it. Since this direct awareness is masked by our life-long habit of thinking about it, the most common initial experience of those embarking on the path of awakening a higher level of awareness is one of discouragement, thinking (with their ordinary mind) that they have had no positive results that they have noticed.

If this corresponds to your experience, take heart and know that you are in good company, not only at this disjointed time in which we are living but perhaps for all past times as well. That is why I am sharing with you the wise counsel attributed to one of the greatest Tibetan Masters, Guru Padmasambhava, who lived in what we call the 9th century, and who evidently had the same problem with his discouraged students. Listen carefully: it is a very subtle teaching about a level of awareness that we can come to know when our sensitivity is heightened by a relaxed but vigilant attention, and the ordinary commentary of the mind is stilled.

The Awakening of Awareness
Guru Padmasambhava

How can you then speak of not understanding the
    nature of the mind?
Moreover, since you are meditating without finding
    anything there to meditate upon,
How can you say that your meditation does not go well?

Since your own manifest intrinsic awareness is just this,
How can you say that you cannot find your own mind?

This mind is just that which is thinking;
And yet, although you have searched (for the thinker),
    how can you say that you do not find him?

With respect to this, nowhere does there exist the one
    who is the cause of (mental) activity.
And yet, since activity exists, how can you say that such
    activity does not arise?

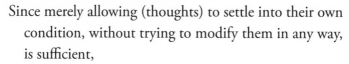

Since merely allowing (thoughts) to settle into their own
  condition, without trying to modify them in any way,
  is sufficient,
How can you say that you are not able to do anything
  with regard to them?

Since clarity, awareness and emptiness are inseparable
  and are spontaneously self-perfected,
How can you say that nothing is accomplished by your
  practice?

Since (intrinsic awareness) is self-originating and
  spontaneously self-perfecting without any antecedent
  causes or conditions,
How can you say that you are not able to accomplish
  anything by your efforts?

Since the arising of discursive thoughts and their being
  liberated occur simultaneously,
How can you say that you are unable to apply the
  antidote?

Since your own immediate awareness is just this,
How can you say that you do not know anything with
  regard to it?

Note that the preceding exchange expounds the Dzogchen view,
as recorded in *Self-Liberation Through Seeing with Naked Awareness* (John Myrdhin Reynolds, Snow Lion, 2000, p. 13-14).

APPENDIX

Al Gore's Nobel Peace Prize Acceptance Speech

Your Majesties, Your Royal Highnesses, Honorable members of the Norwegian Nobel Committee, Excellencies, Ladies and Gentlemen.

I have a purpose here today. It is a purpose I have tried to serve for many years. I have prayed that God would show me a way to accomplish it.

Sometimes, without warning, the future knocks on our door with a precious and painful vision of what might be. One hundred and nineteen years ago, a wealthy inventor read his own obituary, mistakenly published years before his death. Wrongly believing the inventor had just died, a newspaper printed a harsh judgment of his life's work, unfairly labeling him "The Merchant of Death" because of his invention—dynamite. Shaken by this condemnation, the inventor made a fateful choice to serve the cause of peace.

Seven years later, Alfred Nobel created this prize and the others that bear his name.

Seven years ago tomorrow, I read my own political obituary in a judgment that seemed to me harsh and mistaken—if not premature. But that unwelcome verdict also brought a precious if painful gift: an opportunity to search for fresh new ways to serve my purpose.

Unexpectedly, that quest has brought me here. Even though I fear my words cannot match this moment, I pray what I am feeling in my heart will be communicated clearly enough that those who hear me will say, "We must act."

The distinguished scientists with whom it is the greatest honor of my life to share this award have laid before us a choice between two different futures—a choice that to my ears echoes the words of an ancient prophet: "Life or death, blessings or curses. Therefore, choose life, that both thou and thy seed may live."

We, the human species, are confronting a planetary emergency—a threat to the survival of our civilization that is gathering ominous and destructive potential even as we gather here. But there is hopeful news as well: we have the ability to solve this crisis and avoid the worst—though not all—of its consequences, if we act boldly, decisively and quickly.

However, despite a growing number of honorable exceptions, too many of the world's leaders are still best described in the words Winston Churchill applied to those who ignored Adolf Hitler's threat: "They go on in strange paradox, decided only to be undecided, resolved to be irresolute, adamant for drift, solid for fluidity, all powerful to be impotent."

So today, we dumped another 70 million tons of global-warming pollution into the thin shell of atmosphere surrounding our planet, as if it were an open sewer. And tomorrow, we will dump a slightly larger amount, with the cumulative concentrations now trapping more and more heat from the sun.

As a result, the earth has a fever. And the fever is rising. The experts have told us it is not a passing affliction that will heal by itself. We asked for a second opinion. And a third. And a fourth. And the consistent conclusion, restated with increasing alarm, is that something basic is wrong.

We are what is wrong, and we must make it right.

Last September 21, as the Northern Hemisphere tilted away from the sun, scientists reported with unprecedented distress that the North Polar ice cap is "falling off a cliff." One study estimated that it could be completely gone during summer in less than 22 years. Another new study, to be presented by U.S. Navy researchers later this week, warns it could happen in as little as 7 years. Seven years from now.

In the last few months, it has been harder and harder to misinterpret the signs that our world is spinning out of kilter. Major cities in North and South America, Asia and Australia are nearly out of water due to massive droughts and melting glaciers. Desperate farmers are losing their livelihoods. Peoples in the frozen Arctic and on low-lying Pacific islands are planning evacuations of places they have long called home. Unprecedented wildfires have forced a half million people from their homes in one country and caused a national emergency that almost brought down the government in another. Climate refugees have migrated into areas already inhabited by people with different cultures, religions, and traditions, increasing the potential for conflict. Stronger storms in the Pacific and Atlantic have threatened whole cities. Millions have been displaced by massive flooding in South Asia, Mexico, and 18 countries in Africa. As temperature extremes have increased, tens of thousands have lost their lives. We are recklessly burning and clearing our forests and driving more and more species into extinction. The very web of life on which we depend is being ripped and frayed.

We never intended to cause all this destruction, just as Alfred Nobel never intended that dynamite be used for waging war. He had hoped his invention would promote human progress. We shared that same worthy goal when we began burning massive quantities of coal, then oil and methane.

Even in Nobel's time, there were a few warnings of the likely consequences. One of the very first winners of the Prize in chemistry worried that, "We are evaporating our coal mines into the air." After performing 10,000 equations by hand, Svante Arrhenius calculated that the earth's average temperature would increase by many degrees if we doubled the amount of CO_2 in the atmosphere.

Seventy years later, my teacher, Roger Revelle, and his colleague, Dave Keeling, began to precisely document the increasing CO_2 levels day by day. But unlike most other forms of pollution, CO_2 is invisible, tasteless, and odorless, which has helped keep the truth about what it is doing to our climate out of sight and out of mind. Moreover, the catastrophe now threatening us is unprecedented—and we often confuse the unprecedented with the improbable.

We also find it hard to imagine making the massive changes that are now necessary to solve the crisis. And when large truths are genuinely inconvenient, whole societies can, at least for a time, ignore them. Yet as George Orwell reminds us: "Sooner or later a false belief bumps up against solid reality, usually on a battlefield."

In the years since this prize was first awarded, the entire relationship between humankind and the earth has been radically transformed. And still, we have remained largely oblivious to the impact of our cumulative actions.

Indeed, without realizing it, we have begun to wage war on the earth itself. Now, we and the earth's climate are locked in a relationship familiar to war planners: "Mutually assured destruction."

More than two decades ago, scientists calculated that nuclear war could throw so much debris and smoke into the air that it would block life-giving sunlight from our atmosphere, causing a "nuclear winter." Their eloquent warnings here in Oslo helped galvanize the world's resolve to halt the nuclear arms race.

Now science is warning us that if we do not quickly reduce the global warming pollution that is trapping so much of the heat our planet normally radiates back out of the atmosphere, we are in danger of creating a permanent "carbon summer."

As the American poet Robert Frost wrote, "Some say the world will end in fire; some say in ice." Either, he notes, "would suffice."

But neither need be our fate. It is time to make peace with the planet.

We must quickly mobilize our civilization with the urgency and resolve that has previously been seen only when nations mobilized for war. These prior struggles for survival were won when leaders found words at the 11th hour that released a mighty surge of courage, hope and readiness to sacrifice for a protracted and mortal challenge.

These were not comforting and misleading assurances that the threat was not real or imminent; that it would affect others but not ourselves; that ordinary life might be lived even in the presence of extraordinary threat; that Providence could be trusted to do for us what we would not do for ourselves.

No, these were calls to come to the defense of the common future. They were calls upon the courage, generosity and strength of entire peoples, citizens of every class and condition who were ready to stand against the threat once asked to do so. Our enemies in those times calculated that free people would not rise to the challenge; they were, of course, catastrophically wrong.

Now comes the threat of climate crisis—a threat that is real, rising, imminent, and universal. Once again, it is the 11th hour. The penalties for ignoring this challenge are immense and growing, and at some near point would be unsustainable and unrecoverable. For now we still have the power to choose our fate, and the remaining question is only this: Have we the will to act vigorously and in time, or will we remain imprisoned by a dangerous illusion?

Mahatma Gandhi awakened the largest democracy on earth and forged a shared resolve with what he called "Satyagraha"— or "truth force." In every land, the truth—once known—has the power to set us free. Truth also has the power to unite us and bridge the distance between "me" and "we," creating the basis for common effort and shared responsibility.

There is an African proverb that says, "If you want to go quickly, go alone. If you want to go far, go together." We need to go far, quickly.

We must abandon the conceit that individual, isolated, private actions are the answer. They can and do help. But they will not take us far enough without collective action. At the same time, we must ensure that in mobilizing globally, we do not invite the establishment of ideological conformity and a new lock-step "ism."

That means adopting principles, values, laws, and treaties that release creativity and initiative at every level of society in multifold responses originating concurrently and spontaneously.

This new consciousness requires expanding the possibilities inherent in all humanity. The innovators who will devise a new way to harness the sun's energy for pennies or invent an engine that's carbon negative may live in Lagos or Mumbai or Montevideo. We must ensure that entrepreneurs and inventors everywhere on the globe have the chance to change the world.

When we unite for a moral purpose that is manifestly good and true, the spiritual energy unleashed can transform us. The generation that defeated fascism throughout the world in the 1940s found, in rising to meet their awesome challenge, that they had gained the moral authority and long-term vision to launch the Marshall Plan, the United Nations, and a new level of global cooperation and foresight that unified Europe and facilitated the emergence of democracy and prosperity in Germany, Japan, Italy and much of the world. One of their visionary leaders said, "It is time we steered by the stars and not by the lights of every passing ship."

In the last year of that war, you gave the Peace Prize to a man from my hometown of 2000 people, Carthage, Tennessee. Cordell Hull was described by Franklin Roosevelt as the "Father of the United Nations." He was an inspiration and hero to my own father, who followed Hull in the Congress and the U.S. Senate and in his commitment to world peace and global cooperation.

My parents spoke often of Hull, always in tones of reverence and admiration. Eight weeks ago, when you announced this prize, the deepest emotion I felt was when I saw the headline in my hometown paper that simply noted I had won the same prize that Cordell Hull had won. In that moment, I knew what my father and mother would have felt were they alive.

Just as Hull's generation found moral authority in rising to solve the world crisis caused by fascism, so too can we find our greatest opportunity in rising to solve the climate crisis. In the Kanji characters used in both Chinese and Japanese, "crisis" is written with two symbols, the first meaning "danger," the second "opportunity." By facing and removing the danger of the climate crisis, we have the opportunity to gain the moral authority and vision to vastly increase our own capacity to solve other crises that have been too long ignored.

We must understand the connections between the climate crisis and the afflictions of poverty, hunger, HIV-Aids and other pandemics. As these problems are linked, so too must be their solutions. We must begin by making the common rescue of the global environment the central organizing principle of the world community.

Fifteen years ago, I made that case at the "Earth Summit" in Rio de Janeiro. Ten years ago, I presented it in Kyoto. This week, I will urge the delegates in Bali to adopt a bold mandate for a treaty that establishes a universal global cap on emissions and uses the market in emissions trading to efficiently allocate resources to the most effective opportunities for speedy reductions.

This treaty should be ratified and brought into effect everywhere in the world by the beginning of 2010—two years sooner than presently contemplated. The pace of our response must be accelerated to match the accelerating pace of the crisis itself.

Heads of state should meet early next year to review what was accomplished in Bali and take personal responsibility for addressing this crisis. It is not unreasonable to ask, given the gravity of our circumstances, that these heads of state meet every three months until the treaty is completed.

We also need a moratorium on the construction of any new generating facility that burns coal without the capacity to safely trap and store carbon dioxide.

And most important of all, we need to put a price on carbon—with a CO_2 tax that is then rebated back to the people, progressively, according to the laws of each nation, in ways that shift the burden of taxation from employment to pollution. This is by far the most effective and simplest way to accelerate solutions to this crisis.

The world needs an alliance—especially of those nations that weigh heaviest in the scales where earth is in the balance. I salute Europe and Japan for the steps they've taken in recent years to meet the challenge, and the new government in Australia, which has made solving the climate crisis its first priority.

But the outcome will be decisively influenced by two nations that are now failing to do enough: the United States and China. While India is also growing fast in importance, it should be absolutely clear that it is the two largest CO_2 emitters—most of all, my own country—that will need to make the boldest moves, or stand accountable before history for their failure to act.

Both countries should stop using the other's behavior as an excuse for stalemate and instead develop an agenda for mutual survival in a shared global environment.

These are the last few years of decision, but they can be the first years of a bright and hopeful future if we do what we must. No one should believe a solution will be found without effort, without cost, without change. Let us acknowledge that if we wish to redeem squandered time and speak again with moral authority, then these are the hard truths:

The way ahead is difficult. The outer boundary of what we currently believe is feasible is still far short of what we actually must do. Moreover, between here and there, across the unknown, falls the shadow.

That is just another way of saying that we have to expand the boundaries of what is possible. In the words of the Spanish poet, Antonio Machado, "Pathwalker, there is no path. You must make the path as you walk."

We are standing at the most fateful fork in that path. So I want to end as I began, with a vision of two futures—each a palpable possibility—and with a prayer that we will see with vivid clarity the necessity of choosing between those two futures, and the urgency of making the right choice now.

The great Norwegian playwright, Henrik Ibsen, wrote, "One of these days, the younger generation will come knocking at my door."

The future is knocking at our door right now. Make no mistake, the next generation will ask us one of two questions. Either they will ask: "What were you thinking; why didn't you act?"

Or they will ask instead: "How did you find the moral courage to rise and successfully resolve a crisis that so many said was impossible to solve?"

We have everything we need to get started, save perhaps political will, but political will is a renewable resource.

So let us renew it, and say together: "We have a purpose. We are many. For this purpose we will rise, and we will act."

December 10, 2007, Oslo, Norway

Recommended Viewing

AN INCONVENIENT TRUTH. Featuring Al Gore, a film directed by Davis Guggenheim, produced by Laurie David, Lawrence Bender, and Scott Z. Burns.

THE 11th HOUR. Starring Leonardo DiCaprio, Mikhail Gorbechev, Paul Hawken, Stephen Hawking, and William McDonough, directed by Leila Conners Peterson and Nadia Conners, produced by Adam Lewis, Pierre Senizergues, and Irmelin DiCaprio. Produced and narrated by Leonardo DiCaprio.

WHAT THE BLEEP DO WE KNOW? Starring Marlee Matlin, directed by Mark Vicente, Betsy Chasse, and William Arntz, produced by William Arntz and Betsy Chasse.

UFOS: THE SECRET HISTORY. Produced, directed, and narrated by David Cherniak for History Television.

Recommended Reading

Abell, Arthur, *Talks With Great Composers,* Citadel, 1998.

Beath, Andrew, *Consciousness in Action,* Lantern Books, 2005.

Begley, Sharon, *Train Your Mind, Change Your Brain,* Ballantine Books, 2007.

Brown, Lester, *Plan B 3.0, Mobilizing to Save Civilization,* Norton Books, 2008.

Brune, Michael, *Coming Clean: Breaking America's Addiction to Oil and Gas,* Sierra Club/Counterpoint, 2008.

Dalai Lama, "The Peace Within Us" and "My Tibet", *www. dalailama.com.*

Diamond, Jared, *The Last Americans: Environmental Collapse and the End of Civilization,* Harpers, 2003.

Einstein, Albert, *Albert Einstein: The Human Side*, ed. Helen Dukas and Banesh Hoffman, Princeton University Press, 1981. Note that the quotation from Einstein that appears earlier in this book is from a letter of January, 1936.

Fenner, Peter, *Radiant Mind: Awakening Unconditioned Awareness,* Sounds True, 2007.

George, James, *Asking for the Earth: Waking up to the Spiritual/ Ecological Crisis,* Element Books, 1995; Barrytown/Station Hill Press, 2002.

Gore, Al, *An Inconvenient Truth,* Viking Juvenile, 2006.
Earth in the Balance: Ecology and the Human Spirit, Houghton Mifflin, 1992.
Resurgence, No. 242, May–June, 2007.

Goswami, Amit, *The Self-Aware Universe: How Consciousness Creates the Material World,* Tarcher Putnam, 1993.

Gurdjieff, G.I., *Beelzebub's Tales to His Grandson,* Viking Arcana, 1992.

Meetings With Remarkable Men, Viking Arkana, 1983.

Harris, Sam, *The End of Faith,* Norton, 2004.

Hawken, Paul, *Blessed Unrest: How the Largest Movement in the World Came into Being and Why No One Saw It Coming,* Viking Penguin, 2007.

Institute of Noetic Sciences, "The 2007 Shift Report: Evidence of a World Transforming"; "The 2008 Shift Report: Changing the Story of our Future".

Kolbert, Elizabeth, *Field Notes from a Catastrophe: Man, Nature, and Climate Change,* Bloomsbury, 2006.

Krupp, Fred, *Earth: The Sequel: The Race to Reinvent Energy and Stop Global Warming,* W.W. Norton, 2008.

Lappe, Frances Moore, *Getting a Grip: Clarity, Creativity and Courage in a World Gone Mad,* 2007.

Laszlo, Ervin, *Science and the Akashic Field: An Integral Theory of Everything,* Inner Traditions, 2004.

Quantum Shift in the Global Brain, Inner Traditions, 2008.

Lipton, Bruce, *The Biology of Belief,* Elite Books, 2005.

Mack, John, *Passport to the Cosmos,* Crown, 1999.

Macy, Joanna and Fran, "Taking Heart in Tough Times," retreats under this name *in various locations, 2006-2007.*

Macy, Joanna, "Coming Back to Life," a talk originally published in *TIMELINE,* a publication of the *Foundation for Global Community.*

Makhijani, Arjun, *Carbon-Free and Nuclear-Free,* IEER, 2007.

McKibben, Bill, *The End of Nature, Random House,* 1989.

McTaggart, Lynne, *The Intention Experiment, Free Press,* 2007.

Monbiot, George, *Heat: How to Stop the Planet from Burning,* Anchor Canada, 2007.

Nepo, Mark, *The Book of Awakening,* Conari Press, 2000.

Ouspensky, P. D., *In Search of the Miraculous: Fragments of an Unknown Teaching,* Harcourt Brace, 1949.

Needleman, Jacob, *The Inner Journey: Views from the Gurdjieff Work,* Morning Light Press, 2008.

Ravindra, Ravi, *Science and Spirit,* Paragon House, 1991.

Rees, Lord Martin, *Our Final Hour,* Basic Books, 2003.

Reynolds, John Myrdhin, *Self-Liberation Through Seeing with Naked Awareness: An Introduction to the Nature of One's Own Mind from The Profound Teaching of Self-Liberation in the Primordial State of the Peaceful and Wrathful Deities,* Foreword by Namkhai Norbu, Snow Lion Publications, 2000.

Russell, Peter, *Waking up in Time,* Origin Press, 1998.

Schlitz, Marilyn, Cassandra Vieten, and Tina Amorok, *Living Deeply: The Art and Science of Transformation in Everyday Life,* Noetic Books, 2007.

Smolin, Lee, *The Trouble with Physics,* Houghton Mifflin, 2006.

Talbot, Michael, *The Holographic Universe,* Harper Perennial, 1992.

Tikell, Oliver, *Kyoto2,* Zed Books, 2008.

Tolle, Eckhart, *A New Earth: Awakening to Your Life's Purpose,* Penguin, 2008.

Walker, Gabrielle, and Sir David King, *The Hot Topic,* Douglas & McIntyre, 2008.

Wallace, B. Alan, *The Attention Revolution,* Wisdom, 2006.

Weil, Simone, *Waiting for God,* Harper & Row, 1973.

About

Asking for the Earth

The ecological crisis created by our unrelenting and mounting abuse of our planetary home is profoundly indicative of another, more human crisis—an inner and spiritual one. Although these two crises may appear unrelated on the surface, they share a common source in our deep separation from nature and from each other.

James George's seminal and thought-provoking book is essential reading for everyone involved in the quest for solutions to our global and spiritual crises. He skillfully weaves together the seemingly disparate threads of our outer existence—from a Hopi sunrise ceremony and the burning oil wells of Kuwait to an enlightening swim with dolphins—with the wisdom of the interconnectedness of all life and of the profound links between our inner and outer lives.

Venturing further, James George forges powerful links between external ecological issues and the inner worlds of influential spiritual teachers of our century, from Gurdjieff to Chogyal Namkhai Norbu. *Asking for the Earth* is a vital force for change and enlightenment in a dark world.

My old friend James George has written a book in which he shows that the global environmental crisis is actually an expression of inner confusion ... People who seek to make this world a better place to live in will find a great deal here to inspire them.

H.H. THE DALAI LAMA

Riveting, indeed imperative, reading for all those concerned with the future of our planet ... A book that illuminates the human dilemma as none other that I have read.

MAURICE STRONG, Secretary General of the United Nations Conferences on Environment and Development, Stockholm, 1972 and Rio de Janeiro, 1992

James George has written *Asking for the Earth* with a pen dipped alternatively in conscience and compassion. This is not merely a book but a portent.

PAMELA TRAVERS, author of *Mary Poppins*